Love The Life You Live

Reprinted 2000
Reprinted 2001

National Library of Australia

Cataloguing-in Publication Entry:

Hartley, Anne, 1946 –
Love The Life You Live
Bibliography
Includes index
ISBN 0957823703

1. Life Coaching. 2. Self-help. 3. Psychology.

Cover design and typeset by: Michael Shaw 02 9882 3444

Cover picture: Digital Imagery© copyright 2000 PhotoDisc, Inc.

Printed in Australia by: McPhersons Printing Group, Sydney.

Distributed by: Gary Allen Pty Ltd, Sydney

Love The Life You Live

A Ten Step life coaching process

Anne Hartley

This book is dedicated to my daughters
Laura and Lisa.

You are the sunshine in my life.

Acknowledgements

Although one person writes a book, so many others help to create the finished product that you see on the bookshelves. I'd like to thank everyone who helped me create this work:

My daughters Lisa and Laura, for always listening to me, sharing your ideas and just being the wonderful people that you are.

My assistant, Lisa Burnette who did a great editing job, and whose attention to detail helped shape the finished product.

To Jay Ransley for proof-reading.

To all of the life coaches that I've trained, especially Jay Ransley, Marie Farrugia and Marilyn Sullivan, your feedback, support and friendship have made this task easier.

To David, who inspired me and continues to do so.

To Lucy Tomanow, for your advice. Your input is greatly appreciated.

To Michael Shaw, for your design work and patience.

To all of my clients. Thank you for allowing me to share your stories.

Contents

Preface

Have you ever read a self-help book or attended a seminar and been totally excited about the message but not known how to put it into practise in your own life? I remember one time reading a wonderful book that recommended living your purpose. I wanted to do this, I agreed with the message—I just didn't know how.

The information contained in this book has been around for generations. Apart from the way I break down values, I don't think there is anything that hasn't been said before. What is different about this book is the way that I've presented the information. I didn't stumble across the Ten Steps, I actively searched for a straightforward formula that I could use to help me create a better life. What resulted from my search was a process far more powerful than I ever imagined: these Ten Steps have truly transformed my life and the lives of others.

My intention in writing this book is to share what I have learned with you so that you too can create a life that you love.

Introduction

A brief personal history

You know that you've settled for the consolation prize when you achieve all of your goals and they don't make you happy. One day I was sitting in a plush hotel in Auckland. I had just completed a successful tour of speaking engagements and seminars and I had written two very successful books yet all I could think about was how far removed my life was from my original plans. After spending eight years helping other people achieve their dreams, it was time to stop striving and reassess my own.

The worst thing about that time in my life was that I didn't know what I wanted. It was only later as I formalised and worked through the Ten Steps contained in this book for myself that I realised that we always know what we want—only sometimes our dreams get buried beneath a mountain of hurt feelings and disappointments. Rather than face another disappointment or more pain, we delude ourselves into thinking that we don't know what we want. I was no exception.

All I ever wanted from life was to have a happy marriage and healthy babies. A career was my consolation prize for the dream I never achieved. I didn't marry, although I did have children. My first child Lisa, was born in 1968 when I was just twenty-one. My son Robbie was born six years later. Having children as a single mother was not a conscious choice on my part to rebel against society. I desperately wanted to get married—the fathers of my children didn't want to marry me.

Being a single mother in 1968 was socially unacceptable. We were branded 'unmarried mothers' and our children 'illegitimate'. We received no Government pension and very little support. Most girls in my situation at that time were hidden away in homes for unmarried mothers and strongly encouraged to give their babies up for adoption, or they settled for a shotgun wedding.

I was one of the fortunate ones. My parents stood by me and they have always been very supportive of me, even though accepting my choices was difficult for them.

In those days women's wages were much lower than men's wages. The same job opportunities didn't exist for women as for men, and banks rarely lent large sums of money to women for business or home loans. Women were conditioned to believe that they couldn't survive without a man.

I accepted the belief that life would be hard for me and for many years it was a struggle just to survive, until I discovered *The Power of Positive Thinking* by Norman Vincent Peale. That book was the first in a series of books that changed the way I thought, which in turn ultimately changed my life.

By the time I ceased work to be with my second baby a Government pension was available, although it was only a third of what I'd been earning from my last full-time job. My children and I lived on the poverty line with barely enough money for food. I knew I had to find a way to make money fast. I didn't stop and think about what I wanted to do or what I enjoyed, my sole focus was on making enough money to survive. So after assessing my options I started my first business by telling everyone I knew that I was operating a typing service. I didn't have a typewriter or desk to work from when my first assignment, a thesis, arrived two days later. I borrowed money from a girlfriend, hired a typewriter and worked from my kitchen table. Fortunately work poured in from then on, mostly from word-of-mouth recommendations.

I never expected to be self-employed, however between juggling work and children it seemed the obvious choice. Over the next few years I seized every opportunity that came my way, so that by 1980 I was comfortably ensconced in a business with a man I dated occasionally. At last the struggle seemed to be ending and life was comfortable. The business was profitable and my dream of owning a home of my own wasn't very far away.

Three weeks before Christmas 1980 my children and I attended a child's birthday party. When the party ended and all of the guests had gone home, my girlfriend who had hosted the party, Lisa and I relaxed while my youngest son Robbie, then five, played with the birthday girl in her bedroom. Unbeknownst to any of us Robbie slipped out onto the balcony, climbed onto the ledge to fly his paper planes and toppled over—we were five stories high. He died before the ambulance arrived.

Losing a child is like losing your heart. At first you feel numb—then when the shock wears off and the mind begins to accept reality the pain hits you with such intensity you don't feel you'll ever survive. You walk around feeling as if your heart's been smashed into a million pieces and wonder how you are still alive, able to function and manage your daily routine.

On the outside most people think you are okay and handling everything well, inside you feel as if you're falling apart. Your mind plays tricks on you. You dream every night (when you can sleep) a constant dream in which you are trying to save him.

Sometimes you dream that he is still alive and all is as it should be, then you wake up and remember and the pain hits you again—like a sledgehammer. Sometimes you forget and set a place at the table, or go to buy him something, or think to tell him something and then once again you remember and the pain returns. You don't think you'll ever be happy or experience joy again.

If you choose to, you survive—it's a choice though. Over time the pain eases until one day it's gone—if you let it. It reminds me of childbirth, if you have experienced that pain you'll know what I mean. Straight after the birth, when the pain is fresh in your mind, you vow you'll never put yourself through that experience again. Then as time passes the memory diminishes, until next time you find yourself in labour and you wonder how you got back there again. In much the same way you think that you'll never let trivial things upset you again, that you'll never argue with someone you love again, but you forget and you do—but life is never the same, because you've changed.

I learnt from my son's death that I had choices and how I allowed this event to shape my life was up to me. I chose to grow through the experience.

A month after Robbie's death my business partner and I had a major disagreement and our partnership ended. When I left, I walked out with just my office furniture, which was mine before we started the business. I didn't receive any holiday pay or my promised share of the profits. Our joint account proceeds were initially frozen and later released by the bank to my partner, without my permission. Those savings were to be my house deposit.

Although I did get back the money that I originally invested in the business, this came in small monthly instalments, that weren't large enough to live off or to start another business with.

I was in no fit emotional state to return to work as an employee, so the only alternative that I could think of was to start another secretarial service. Without even thinking it through I rented a rather dilapidated shop in an industrial area. As my business grew I added the placement of temporary and permanent office staff to the services we provided. For the first eighteen months business flourished, but as I progressively lost interest it began to struggle. I didn't have the energy or enthusiasm to put into it any more because it wasn't what I really wanted to do. I'd started this business as a reaction to my circumstances, driven by the need for an income. When I became aware that my heart was no longer in it I sold this business.

By this time I was thirty five with thirty six looming on the horizon, and I couldn't understand how far removed my life was from my original goal of a happy marriage and children. I decided that if I couldn't have the marriage and family that I wanted, then I would concentrate on raising my daughter Lisa and on making money. I felt this would give my life meaning. What really happened was I gave myself another consolation prize.

I returned to work in the investment industry in 1982. All of my working life I've attended courses, studied and continually added to my skills and this time was no exception. Financial planning was a fairly new industry at that time and very few women were licensed to give advice. Fortunately I was. I was offered a position setting up and running a women's investment advisory service and I later took over a franchise of this business. I presented seminars on investing to the public and was regularly interviewed by the media. Before long I was writing columns on money matters for major magazines and newspapers. This apparent success didn't just happen—I made it a reality by working hard, studying, meditating, saying affirmations and visualising to help me achieve my goals.

During this time I re-established contact with a man that I gone out with in my twenties and we fell in love again. For me this was the first time I'd ever really been in love (although I thought I'd been before). We had a very close, loving relationship for a long period of time, but in keeping with my belief that I could only have the consolation prize I had chosen a man who was afraid of making a commitment. When I discovered that I was pregnant again, at the age of forty, our relationship came under a lot of pressure and eventually changed. We wanted different things—I wanted marriage, he didn't know what he wanted. When our daughter Laura was two he left both our lives and decided not to see either of us again.

The pain of that loss touched me deeply. It wasn't just the loss of someone I loved but also the loss of the dream, that I knew would never be—but life goes on and I had a child to take care of. Whenever I had previously felt hurt or life became too tough I would throw myself into my work and this time was no exception. It was during this time that my first book, *Financially Free,* was released and it became an immediate best-seller.

Following the success of that book, the pressure on my time increased. I still had my business to run, I was trying to be a full-time mum, as well as a professional speaker travelling around Australia and New Zealand. I had regular spots on TV and radio. I had all the success that I thought would make me happy and it meant nothing to me. I wasn't chasing my dream, I'd gone after the consolation prize again. I had actively sought public recognition hoping that would fill the void within me; it didn't. I learnt first hand that you can never get enough of what you don't want.

At that time I wasn't ready to do the work that I do today. Intellectually I had the knowledge but emotionally I felt like a fraud because my life didn't always work. In those days I still expected to 'arrive' one day, little knowing that life is a process and there is nowhere to arrive to and that no one has the perfect life.

It had however become clear to me that I needed to change my life. I gave up my financial planning business and started a new business that I ran from home but it was a financial disaster from the beginning. I'd acted on my emotions rather than researching sufficiently and I should have closed the business after a few months, but because I hate to give up I struggled on for twelve months, losing more and more money.

Instead of having more time to relax and spend with my youngest daughter Laura I ended up having less time and I was constantly stressed. The next few years passed in a haze of confusion. My intentions were good but there was still a lot I needed to learn about myself and about life. My eldest daughter Lisa was working and independent by this time and my youngest child was still very young, although now at school. I wanted to be at home with Laura, but I was bored, I liked the stimulation of work and I needed more money, but I'd lost my confidence and I felt like a failure. I went from being successful to being plagued with money worries, so much so that I ended up taking a part-time bookkeeping job because I needed the income. I went from being paid $150 an hour for a consultation (and thousands for a talk) to just $17 an hour, it was an incredible blow to my ego. The conditions at the part-time job were so bad—the desks were propped up with milk crates and the bins were old oil drums. The kitchen was so filthy that I had to sterilise everything with boiling water before I could make a cup of coffee.

While on the outside things appeared bleak, this time in my life motivated me to do the work that I do today. Life often presents our greatest opportunities under the guise of problems and I was aware that I'd created my success before and I knew I could do it again. However, this time I decided I wanted a formula, a step-by-step process that I could use to create what I wanted, so that I wouldn't keep making the same mistakes. I knew that there were others just like me and if I could make it work for myself, then I could help others going through similar struggles.

Once again I had a purpose and as I experimented with and lived the Ten Steps my life began to flow and change for the better. I experienced synchronicity where the right people and the right opportunities seem to appear out of the blue—the reality is that we attract them when we are congruent.

One day someone I didn't even know rang and asked me if I'd be interested in ghost writing a financial book for one of his clients, and believe me the pay was a lot better than $17 an hour. I agreed and although this wasn't my ideal work, I enjoyed it. Out of the blue my accountant recommended me to someone else who wanted a book written. I ghost wrote three books in all and adapted two of Suze Orman's books for the Australian market. This work wasn't another consolation prize, it was a stepping stone, a short-term solution that paid good money for a skill I'd developed. I knew without the worry of how to survive financially that I'd be able to focus on creating a business that I really loved. I was always very clear about this. I changed the way I thought, spoke and acted and I started living according to my values and as I did this my circumstances changed.

During the first twelve months of working with the Ten Steps I quadrupled my income. Although I'd made good money previously the change this time was consistent. I no longer experienced the fluctuations in income that I used to experience even with financial planning.

Over the next twelve months I achieved more personal goals than I had in the previous five years, I now wanted to help others who were lost and confused as I had been. I began working as a life coach and was prepared to work for nothing if I had to—I was so passionate about the Ten Steps. Fortunately I didn't have to as the Ten Steps worked for my clients as well as they did for me. Twelve months later four people within a space of a few weeks, asked if I would train them to be life coaches. I ran my first life coach training course as a trial That first group of eight women who attended my life coach training program are the most wonderful, supportive, loving group of women you could ever meet; some of them I still speak with every week. The people that I now attract and work with are very different from those I once attracted.

My life today is far removed from what I originally imagined, but I can say quite honestly that I love my life, I feel so blessed. I receive so much love and appreciation on a daily basis from my family, my friends, clients and students and so much fulfillment from my work. I love what is now, and I love what the future holds for me. You too can create a life that you love—when you choose it for yourself.

The Ten Steps contained within this book have transformed my life and the lives of many of my clients and life coaches whom I've trained. You too can transform your life, the choice is yours.

Step One

Break free from the influence of the tribe

Whatever you're ready for is ready for you.
—Mark Victor Hansen

One day I was walking with a neighbour when she said to me, 'What I really want is to own my own business selling materials, and I want to run it from home'. She went into great detail telling me exactly what she wanted and how she would run this business. She also told me all the reasons why she couldn't have what she wanted, most of them related to loss of security if she gave up a well-paying part-time job, and possible problems obtaining Council approval. Sally is passionate about craft work and is very talented, she creates beautiful dolls, quilts and works of art.

Over the next few days I thought about Sally's dream and came up with some ways to overcome the obstacles she'd mentioned as well as some practical ideas for marketing this business without spending a lot of money. My plan enabled Sally to continue working at her part-time job until the business could support her. I was excited by the possibilities and looked forward to sharing my ideas with her. However, my suggestions didn't meet with the enthusiasm I expected. Sally's only response was to say, 'You make it sound so easy'.

Needless to say Sally didn't act on any of my suggestions, or even investigate the possibilities further. Sally's behaviour is not that uncommon. Many people fail to act on opportunities everyday, and they continue to moan about their lot and that's because they don't believe they can have what they really want. They believe for whatever reason, it may be because of their conditioning or because they have tried before and failed, that life just happens. They believe that good fortune or success is a matter of luck or circumstances outside of their control. The fact is your life is no accident: it is a result of the choices that you've made up to now. Your life tomorrow will be a result of the choices that you make today.

If you were to ask any very young child what they want to be when they grow up you'll usually find they are very clear on what they want to have, and whom they want to be. Sure it's usually fantasy, but with childlike faith they don't stop and think if it's possible, if they are capable, or if they can afford it. As we grow older we often give up our childhood dreams and that's usually a natural process of maturity, but what we also give up is our childlike faith and we become 'realistic'. In most cases being 'realistic' is another word for being 'limited'. This usually occurs for a number of reasons, the most common being that we have been told by the tribe so many times that we can't have everything that we want, that we start believing it. Our personal history in most cases has a foundation of beliefs, values and rules that have been inherited from the tribe.

To honour yourself, and to be able to create a life that you love, you need to break free from the influence of the tribe and reassess your core beliefs, values and rules.

Understanding the influences of the tribe

When I talk about 'the tribe', I am referring to people such as family, friends, teachers, workmates, religious group and society as a whole that we are all influenced by. It is from the tribe that you've acquired your beliefs, values and the rules you live by. I am not talking about a cult-type influence and it is not my intention to offend any cultures that honour the tribe. What I am referring to are the everyday influences—the cultural beliefs—that we are all subjected to which may limit your opportunities. When we accept what we are told unquestioningly then we can pass along limiting beliefs, myths and half-truths without even realising it. Some people question the validity of tribal indoctrination as they mature, but others continue to accept it without question. Most are not even aware they are so strongly affected by the tribe.

Whether you've questioned your conditioning or not, it's a rare person who doesn't make decisions without being influenced by what other people think. When you stop reacting, which is what we all do until we become consciously aware, and start thinking about the choices that you make you remain on the same old treadmill with the same old issues often recurring over and over again. When you consciously choose what you want, you have the opportunity to create a different reality.

Julie was confused about her work, she didn't know what she wanted to do. She'd spent twenty years hopping from one career to the other, and was successful in most undertakings although it wasn't long before she lost interest in each new job. She originally started work as a teacher—then became a nurse. When she succeeded in that field, she decided to start all over again and study naturopathy. After studying for four years she came to me for coaching, still unsure of the work she wanted to do. Due to many years of effort, and thousands of dollars invested in studying, Julie had very little time to enjoy the things that were important to her.

When I first began working with Julie I noticed how often she uttered phrases that began with, 'I should', 'I have to' or, 'What will people think?'. These phrases are all indicators that the opinions of others were influencing her choices. So, each time I heard Julie utter one of these phrases I would point it out to her, and she soon became aware how many of her choices were based on what others thought of her. As Julie reassessed her values and rules and made a conscious choice to break free from the tribe she was offered a job that enabled her to utilise most of her skills. This she described as her 'dream job' which met every requirement she had listed in her 'dream job wish list', and the added bonus was that now she was paid extremely well.

When Julie took the focus off confusion and focused more on creating beliefs, values and rules that were of her choosing, the job manifested of its own accord.

There is nothing wrong with taking advice from someone whose opinion you value, however, you know you are being unduly influenced by the tribe if you find yourself continually saying any of the following statements:

What will people think?

I can't go out looking like this.

People will think I'm an idiot if I change my mind again.

I'll look like a fool.

You must think I'm awful.

But what will people say?

When your life choices are influenced by the tribe it's not uncommon to need to appear more prosperous than you really are. This usually involves 'keeping up with the Jones' and living beyond your means. I have met many people who live in two worlds, in their business or professional lives they appear outwardly successful, dress well, drive a nice car, speak well and generally portray the image of someone who is prosperous and successful. However, their personal life tells a different story—while they may live in nice accommodation, it's often rented, they have little money to spend, and a lot of their personal time is spent talking about their struggles.

I've also met many single women who believe that finding a husband will solve their problems. They want this man to support them and also achieve all of their goals for them. The tribal rule that a man should be the provider is less prevalent today than it once was, but there are still some who cling to it.

When you are bonded to the tribe all your decisions, rules and values are influenced by what others think of you and these may not necessarily be your own preferences.

Keeping up appearances saps so much of your energy that there's rarely enough left over to create the things that are really important to you.

The problem is that often it's hard to recognise when you are being influenced by others because it's become so natural to act that way. Ten years ago I would have vehemently denied being influenced by the tribe, in fact I would have pointed out all that I had done that was non-conformist. I now realise that so many of my choices were influenced by what others thought of me because I was trying to prove something to others.

To create the life you want, you need to break free from the influence of the tribe and to do this, you need to separate emotionally from it. This does not necessarily mean leaving the tribe, although some do. Separating emotionally allows you to be free to make your own decisions based on who you are and what you want from life—not based on what you are told or what other people will think of you. It also requires you to reassess your beliefs, rules and values and choose ones that will help you to create a life you love.

Beliefs

Your beliefs are a direct result of conditioning—until you make conscious choices as to whether they are valid for you or not.

As a child you were constantly bombarded with messages from your family, teachers and society as a whole. These messages were passed on verbally and non-verbally and have become a part of your belief system. These beliefs dictate whether you'll make money easily or whether you'll struggle; whether you believe you are clever, stupid, or just average; helpful or lazy; kind or selfish; hard to get on with or easy to get on with; lovable or hard to love. These labels are not who you are unless you choose to believe them. Being called stupid doesn't make you stupid; it just tells you something about the person who is calling you stupid.

As a child you also made judgements by observing the world around you and how those close to you responded to life's challenges. You will have observed how your family achieved their goals, if they even had goals, whether they struggled or achieved their desires easily. All of these observations will have had a profound influence on your life and the choices that you make today. Your core beliefs (what you really believe at a subconscious level) are what influence your choices—not how positive you pretend to be.

The easiest way to uncover your core beliefs is to listen to the words that you say. I discovered one of my core beliefs while shopping one day with my youngest daughter Laura, who was four at the time. Like most young children, Laura would ask me to buy her something every time we went to the shops. On this particular day I responded to Laura's request by saying, 'You can't have everything that you want'.

It's not uncommon to hear parents say this. It was something that had been said to me as a child and I in turn said the same thing to my children without thinking. This is exactly how tired worn-out phrases, which don't even apply to life as we know it today, get passed on from one generation to the next. Although I consider myself a very positive person and I tell my children many times that they can have everything that they want, the reality was that when my daughter asked for it, she was told that she couldn't have everything she wanted. What I found to be so incredible was that I had been making that statement for more than twenty years, and I wasn't consciously aware of it. The only reason I became aware on this occasion was because another shopper who was standing in front of me at the cash register turned around and said, 'Don't children today want everything'. Her comment brought my own words to my attention.

I am not recommending that you give your children everything that they ask for in order to reinforce positive beliefs. Children need to learn patience, know there are boundaries and respect money, this is how we can teach them to create for themselves. However, at the same time as parents we need to consciously listen to what we say so that we do not confuse our children by giving them mixed messages.

We all grow up hearing mixed messages and some of these messages you may have unconsciously chosen to believe over all others. These become core beliefs which influence all your choices and actions. We all have core beliefs on a whole range of subjects which dictate how much we can have; what we can do; how much we will be supported; and how hard or easy our lives will be.

You can discover what some of your core beliefs are simply by looking at your life. For instance, do you get what you want easily, or is life a struggle for you? Do you always have enough money, or is there never enough? Do you always land on your feet, or do things always go wrong for you? Your patterns, struggles and recurring issues are all indicators of your core beliefs.

Limiting beliefs are ones that make it hard for you to create the life you really want. The good news is that what happened in your past doesn't have to be a part of your future. Your future is shaped now, in this very moment, by the choices that you make today. You are always free to change your core beliefs at any time like Sue and John did.

Sue and her husband John lost their home, cars, jobs and lifestyle when their business failed. Unable to obtain work they were forced to live on unemployment benefits.

Sue's Story

We had to make such dramatic changes to the way we lived, at first we were completely devastated by the whole experience. It was sad enough losing our home of twenty years, but the worst thing was that we lost hope.

Everyone we knew sympathised and told us to apply for Government housing, but all this advice did was reinforce the belief that it was too late to start again. We felt like failures. We were in our mid fifties and our children were still at school. The future didn't look particularly appealing.

For two years John tried to find a job, attending interviews nearly every week without any success. One day when we had trouble scraping together enough money to pay the electricity bill and had barely enough money for food we knew we were fed up with being poor. We called a family meeting and decided that as we had already hit rock bottom things could only get better—we had nothing to lose by going back into business for ourselves again. We decided to open a take-away food business.

We had no money but pain is a great motivator and we weren't going to let that minor detail stop us. There was a shop in our town that had been vacant for months so John asked the owner to help us. He asked for three months free rent and said that if at the end of that period we were able to make our business viable we would be happy to sign a lease—the owner agreed.

We had no refrigerator to store drinks, so I asked the drink company to supply one—they agreed. Some people refused our requests but we just kept asking until we found someone who said 'yes'. It wasn't easy but it was better than the alternative. The children, John and I painted the shop, and we were able to get free carpet from a movie theatre that was looking for someone to take it away. We also managed to gather other furniture and fittings in the same way. We rang our old suppliers and asked if they would supply us with minimal food on credit, and they agreed. A signwriter provided signs at no charge when we offered to advertise his business on our car. Our business has flourished and within a short period of time we were self-sufficient again.

We started thinking about buying a home, but finding a deposit at our age seemed a big stretch, so we bought land that we could afford in a rural area, and slowly built our home. Living in the country was our dream even during the prosperous years.

We wouldn't go back to our old lifestyle now. It nearly killed us when we lost our home but we love our new home even more. If we had listened to what everyone told us, we would have given up hope, and that would mean that we would still have been dependent on a Government handout.

Your actions are always influenced by your core beliefs, which usually originate from the tribe. However, you have the power to change your core beliefs at any time. I have covered how you can change limiting beliefs in the next step.

Rules

Your rules are the standards of behaviour that you find acceptable or unacceptable and just like beliefs and values, rules are generally not a conscious choice but are a result of your conditioning. To discover what your rules are, and most people have more than they think, just take note of how often you say the words 'have to', 'should' and 'must'. These words indicate the rules that you live by, or feel you should live by and these rules influence all of your decisions.

Another way to describe rules is our expectations. The expectations that we place upon others and ourselves and on what we need, will play a large part in how happy or unhappy we will be.

I went on holiday at one time to a beautiful island. The accommodation we stayed in was good but not as luxurious as the resort nearby. The island however was beautiful: just to sit on the beach and watch the sunrise or sunset was magical. Julie who accompanied me wasn't happy just doing this. Instead of enjoying her surroundings and the beauty of nature, she would watch the rich people staying at the nearby resort and envy how they lived. She constantly compared herself to others who were more prosperous than she was and found herself, and her lifestyle lacking. Julie had constant money problems and wondered why, when she worked so hard to achieve her goals, she never seemed to get what she really wanted. It wouldn't be so hard for Julie to understand if she realised how her rules can make her happy or unhappy.

Our perception of success or happiness is dictated by our rules, and my friend's rules implied that in order to be successful and happy she had to live affluently. These rules not only prevented her from being happy, they also limited her opportunities. The more rigid your rules, the harder it will be for you to achieve your goals, and to be happy with them when you do. Tony Robbins says, 'The truth is that nothing has to happen in order for you to feel good'. When you can make this rule valid for you, then you can create anything.

A lot of people live by the 'I'll be happy when...' rule. They believe they will be happy when they find the right person to share their life with, when they find the right job, when they buy a home of their own, have children, or have more money. When you live by the 'I'll be happy when...' rule you spend your life striving but never arriving, it won't matter how much you achieve, it will never be enough.

Years ago when I was looking for direction in my own life I consulted an astrologer and we became quite friendly. Later when I bought my home I invited her to my house-warming party. She rang to say she couldn't attend and took the opportunity to berate me for buying a house. She said, 'Anne, how could you buy a house? You know as well as any-one the financial disasters that are going to happen. How could you take on a mortgage at this time?' The disaster that she referred to were predictions of the collapse of our entire financial system, as well as a tidal wave hitting Sydney close to where I live. Needless to say none of these dire predictions came to pass. It was one time when I was glad that I followed my own rules rather than hers. I have a rule that has served me well though, and that is I never make any decisions based on fear.

There is nothing good or bad about rules; they are a guide just like your values. Some rules will make you happy, other rules will make you unhappy. However, the more rules you have, the harder you make life for yourself and for those around you. Less 'shoulds' in your life means less stress.

Breaking free

Our life crises tell us that we need to break free of old beliefs, values and rules that no longer serve who we are today. These beliefs and the combined energy of a tribe that creates and sustains them can be phenomenal.

In her book, *Anatomy of the Spirit*[1], author Caroline Myss describes the polio epidemic of the 1930s and 1940s as an expression of tribal energy. In 1929 the US economy crashed and the Great Depression began. At this time, Americans, from all walks of life, described themselves as being 'crippled' by this disaster. Shortly afterwards, the polio epidemic struck, and people were literally crippled. What's more, the tribal energy of fear struck the most susceptible, its children.

During this period the American people also elected a crippled president to office. It took the tribal event of World War II. to restore America's belief in itself as a nation and world leader.

Caroline Myss also says[1], 'Seen symbolically, our life crises tell us that we need to break free of beliefs that no longer serve our personal development. Once we accept personal responsibility for even one area of our lives, we can never again use 'tribal reasoning' to excuse our behaviour'.

There will always be someone willing to tell you what you can't do or can't have, they are merely expressing their beliefs and fears about what is possible for them. And, there will always be others who follow their beliefs with passion, and achieve their dreams despite the odds, others like David.

David's story

It was a lovely summer day however, I was feeling off colour and lacking in energy so I decided to call in at my doctor's office on my way home from work. I'd had some blood tests carried out a few weeks beforehand and I wanted to get the results.

As I waited other patients kept going in to the doctor's office in front of me. As many of them had arrived after me I soon became annoyed. After an hour I was begin-

ning to fume. Finally when all the other patients had left the doctor called me into his office.

I was about to complain about the appalling service when my doctor said he'd left me until last as he wanted to spend as much time with me as possible as he had bad news. My doctor said, 'Your blood tests reveal that you are HIV Positive'.

Those words opened a trap door and I felt as if I had fallen into the bowels of the earth, everything around me was black. It took an hour before I could summon up the courage to walk out the door of the doctor's office.

Although it was still daylight as I walked home, I was lost in a black fog. I felt as if I ran into everyone I knew that night but I couldn't even stop and say hello, smile or wave. I simply put my head down and ignored everyone.

That night was followed by three years of darkness where I was obsessed with death. I was in total conflict—when I wasn't thinking about dying I vowed this disease wouldn't kill me and all of my energy was directed towards healing.

The night of my diagnosis I gave up all alcohol and didn't touch a drop for four years. I researched how vitamins can boost the immune system and became fanatical about supplements, for awhile taking every vitamin possible.

All my income went on vitamins and health products. I went totally overboard, exercising to the extreme. Even though I was fighting to change the belief that AIDS would kill me, AIDS controlled my life totally.

During that time a lot of fear and controversy surrounded the AIDS virus and people with the disease were social outcasts. I told only four people who were closest to me.

I participated in every experimental drug trial possible and managed to delay the onset of full-blown AIDS for eight years. Most times the effect of these drugs was worse than the disease itself. One drug tasted hideous, like melted down metal and that taste stayed with me all day long contaminating the taste of everything I ate and drank. This was followed by headaches so excruciating that I had to be hospitalised for ten days and placed on a morphine drip. I decided the price was too high and stopped taking the drug—my health improved immediately.

Another drug caused ingrown toenails. The skin of my toes actually grew over my nails and resulted in pain so severe I could barely walk. As the drug trials only made me worse I eventually went off all experimental drugs and continued with the standard drug cocktail available to all AIDS patients.

Apart from the side effects of drugs I never succumbed to any of the illnesses suffered by AIDS victims. My biggest problem was my immune system, or more correctly my lack of one. The virus breaks down the immune system so that the body's natural defence system is annihilated. A simple thing like a common cold can kill an AIDS victim. The body's immune system is measured by a CD4 count, a normal healthy person's count would be around twelve hundred. Mine fell as low as forty three.

I was committed to remaining healthy and all of my actions reinforced the belief that I could beat AIDS. I read many books, among them Louise Hay's, You Can Heal Your Life. Following the advice in that book I affirmed daily, 'My body is strong and healthy. I have a strong immune system'. I expected instant results and when I wasn't instantly healed I assumed that affirmations didn't work. I now realise that affirmations are powerful, but they are one part of the process. The fact was that I was still alive and healthy fourteen years after that first diagnosis, when practically everyone else I knew who was diagnosed at that time had died.

Still committed to being completely healed I knew I had to give up full-time work. I had a high-pressure job and lived with constant stress. I had no energy and began to fall asleep in meetings and I knew that if I wasn't careful this stress could kill me before the disease did.

After sixteen years of living with AIDS I decided that I needed more help. I was tired of waiting to die. I just wanted to get on with my life and start setting and achieving goals again.

When I first began working with the Ten Steps new opportunities came my way and my investments in the stock market grew. Then one day the market fell and my investments along with it. I'd ignored my own intuition and followed the advice of a broker, believing he was the 'expert'. I had to sell all of my good shares to pay the margin calls on the poorer performing stocks. I lost a tremendous amount of money, the only security I had. I felt devastated and was diagnosed with suspected pneu-

monia and was hospitalised, but it was only a temporary setback.

At first my focus was entirely on achieving material goals, but as I became increasingly independent of the tribe and reassessed my beliefs, values and rules—I changed. I became more tolerant and understanding. While I still choose to achieve my material goals I became aware that making others happy was what made me happy, and I made a point of doing something for someone else everyday.

By late December 1999 my specialist told me that I was immune to nearly all the drugs currently available to AIDS patients that hold off the virus. I commenced taking the last available drug.

I was at a crossroads. I could choose to believe what I was told, that I would soon die. Or, I could choose to create a new reality. I decided that I had nothing to lose by allowing no doubt that I would be totally healed.

I made up a wall chart which showed the AIDS virus shrinking to nothing so that the first words I saw when I opened my eyes each morning were, 'I am completely healed'.

I maintained my daily routine of going to the gym, for walks, taking drug cocktails, vitamins, as well as visualising and meditating. I made sure that all my thoughts, words and actions supported this new belief.

Two months later I went to my specialist for the results of my last blood test, I have one every three months. This time he finally said the words that I waited sixteen years to hear, 'The blood test showed that you now have a zero viral load', which means that the AIDS virus was no longer detectable in my body. My doctor was so overcome he came around to the other side of his desk and hugged me.

Although I was delighted with the news I wasn't really surprised as I always knew it would happen. It just took a little longer than I expected.

AIDS is not a death sentence, it never has been. I firmly believe my mental attitude, and the fact that I fought all the way, contributed to my conquering the disease.

Working with the Ten Steps was like discovering the missing piece of a jigsaw puzzle. They helped bring together all that I'd learnt over the past sixteen years so that I could heal myself.

David is one of the most inspirational people I know and constantly reminds me that anything is possible when we choose to break free from the influence of tribe, and create new beliefs about what is possible.

Step Two

Know who you want to be

Often people attempt to live their lives backward: they try to have more things, or more money, in order to do more of what they want so they will be happier.

The way it actually works is the reverse. You must first be who you really are, then, do what you need to do, in order to have what you want.

—Margaret Young

We all need a reason for living and the stronger the reason, the more motivation we have. Many think of their life's purpose as something they want to achieve. Some people say, 'I want to help others' or, 'I want to teach'. These are very valid goals, but they are only one part of your life's purpose. Your goals are not you. Your purpose is the person you choose to be, and you demonstrate this choice through your actions on a daily basis. Who you choose to be is the code of honour that you choose to live by.

In order to create the life you really want and to be happy with your choices you need to think first and foremost about who you want to be. Do you want to be kind or generous? Loving or passionate? I call these your *being* values—living according to these values is your life's purpose.

Knowing and living according to your *being* values has a twofold benefit. Firstly by making a commitment to demonstrate your *being* values on a daily basis you have a very clear code of ethics and standards to live by; this makes it easier for you respond positively to the ups and downs of daily living. Secondly, by choosing to act on these values you break the pattern of reacting, and this is how you change old beliefs and create new beliefs about yourself.

Let me give you an example of how this works. If a person cuts you off just as you are about to drive into a parking spot, think about how you want to *act*. If you *reacted* you might be tempted to make a rude gesture, give them a black look, scream abuse, mutter to yourself or complain about their rudeness to whomever is in the car with you—you could let another person's actions spoil your day. Or, you can act like the person you choose to be and look upon this incident as an opportunity for you to demonstrate who you want to be, that could be kind and generous. You may feel irritated at first for a short while, but you will have turned a potentially negative experience into something positive and over time as you make new choices in this way you'll feel so good about yourself. Try a similar experiment and see how powerful you feel as a result of choosing how you want to act.

Remember, when you react you give your power away. When you choose to act like the person that you want to be you not only feel good about yourself, you reinforce your chosen belief and you change your perception of the world, and the world in turn changes its perception of you. Everyday you make choices, you can choose to act like a victim who has no control over what happens to her, or you can choose to be powerful, strong, positive, inspirational or kind. You can choose to adopt a value that suits any situation you're in.

Now when you stop and think about it and observe what's happening around you, you'll notice that most people are reacting all of the time. Imagine some of these scenarios and see if you can relate to any of them:

- It's a weekday morning, you have to get to work and get the kids off to school. Your children all have jobs to do but instead of doing them and getting ready for school they watch TV. Fed up you start yelling or you feel stressed before your day really begins.
- You're stuck in traffic and you know you're going to be late. You sit in your car and fume and arrive at your destination feeling stressed.
- Your boss blames you for something that's not your fault and you feel unappreciated and angry. You tell everyone close to you about this event and it spoils your day.

As you experience moments like these you often don't even realise what you're doing, but now you do.

It takes time and some effort to change a habit, however you can do it if you choose to. Just by taking this one simple step of acting like the person you choose to be can dramatically transform your life, even if it was good to begin with.

Choosing who you want to be

I suggest that you split your *being* values into two sets. For the first set choose three values which are the character traits of the person you want to be. Make sure that you choose values that you are prepared to make the effort to live by. These are your life's purpose values and rarely change.

I recommend you choose only three because you want to easily be able to remember them. I once asked a client what his values were and he extracted a piece of paper from his wallet and read off around twelve values to me. This made me realise that if you have to consult a piece of paper, then it's unlikely you will be living those values on a daily basis. You need to know your values intimately because there will be many times when you will have to make a snap decision as to how you wish to respond.

When you've chosen your three most important *being* values write out a code of honour that you commit to live by. This will give you have a very clear standard of behaviour to base future choices and actions upon. You might wonder why you would bother, it's a lot of work and it is. However, it's something that you only have to do once. All of your life you have responded to tribal conditioning and have therefore simply *reacted* for much of your life. Now it's your turn to consciously choose the standards you wish to live by and you need to be very clear about what those are. If for instance you choose to be honest, understand how honest you want to be. Are you prepared to say what you think to everyone even if it means hurting their feelings? Are you prepared to pay all the taxes you legitimately owe? What is your definition of honesty?

Once you've done this don't be too hard on yourself if you forget to act this way sometimes, we all do.

David grasped this concept immediately. When we first started working together David chose to be tolerant and everyday he encountered small opportunities where he could practise being a tolerant person. At one time an elderly lady drove her car very slowly through the shopping centre and held up all the traffic, rather than getting impatient and honking his horn David chose to relax and accept this. Children ran around a restaurant where he was eating a meal, but instead of complaining or asking to be moved to a quieter table he said nothing and relaxed. As a result of this David felt happy and content with himself and increasingly more powerful.

When David's investments failed due to poor advice from his stockbroker he'd been acting like a tolerant person for some time, and this helped him through a difficult period in his life and enabled him to move on. David didn't waste energy blaming, instead he allowed himself to feel devastated for two days before reassessing his priorities and started making new plans. It was at this time that David realised that he focused too much on making money and has since chosen to do more for the community and is happier as a result of his new choices.

The second set of *being* values, again I suggest you choose three, often change as your goals change. These are the traits that you adopt to help you achieve what you want at a given time in your life. In some situations being positive may be the best way to act, in another you may need to be courageous or wise. When you are confronted by a situation ask yourself, 'How would a courageous (or whatever value is appropriate) person act in this situation?', then act accordingly.

At one time I had a built-in cupboard installed in my home. On installation the fitter discovered that one of the doors was the wrong size and took it back, promising the right door would be delivered two days later. That same promise was made and broken five times over a period of two weeks, causing me a lot of inconvenience. There were times when I felt tempted to be extremely rude, then I would ask myself if this is how a kind, loving, generous person would act. These traits are the *being* values that I have chosen for my life's purpose. After a promise was made and broken for the sixth time, I decided to be powerful, and I acted like a powerful person.

I rang the manager and very politely told him that I was going to stay on the phone until we found a way to get my door to me *that day*. I was very pleasant but said, 'I am prepared to work with you on this, but I won't accept being fobbed off any longer. What can I do for you so that you can get my door to me today?' The man was so taken with my approach that we ended up laughing about the matter, although he also knew that I was adamant. Eventually the manager guaranteed that I would get my door that day however, by late afternoon it still hadn't arrived. So I rang the manager again and he promised to deliver the door himself. He drove to my home after work which is a long way from where he lives and he didn't arrive until 8pm, however, he did keep his promise. I don't believe he would have done this if I had been abusive.

I demonstrated to myself that I can have what I want without comprising who I am to obtain it. I can still go back to that company at any time without any feelings of embarrassment that I would have felt if I had 'lost it'. After that experience I decided to add *powerful* to my second set of *being* values.

When fear takes over

At one time I was coaching a client who wanted to buy a specific business. She'd been given a verbal option to buy the business and a date to exercise that option by so that she could raise the necessary capital. In the meantime the business owner accepted an offer from someone else. When my client heard this she was understandably upset and decided to act forcefully. She misrepresented the truth to the owners with the intention of making them feel bad so they would reverse their decision. Her method worked in the short term and she was given one week to arrange finance and lodge a better offer. Her sole focus was on getting what she wanted and she was prepared to manipulate to get it, but in doing so she forgot to act like the person she wanted to be. When she told me about what had happened I asked her to describe the type of person she would like to be. She told me that she'd like others to think of her as a person of integrity, who was honest and responsible—however, she didn't act like the person that she wanted to be, she didn't achieve her goal and she was miserable with the outcome.

Now this is what many people do a lot of the time. They want to be considered honest or some other character trait, however when they look like losing something that's important to them, in other words when they feel fearful, they allow fear or their ego to dictate their actions. Often this means they act contrary to the person they want to be. You only have to look at how some people behave when a marriage or business partnership breaks down to see fear in action. Through her actions my client demonstrated her core belief was that she couldn't have what she really wanted. Every time she acted contrary to the person she wanted to be she reinforced that belief.

Whenever fear dictates your actions you will be disappointed with the result; you may gain the results you desire in the short term but you won't achieve long term satisfaction.

The only way to change a core belief is to act on your *being* values.

Your problems can be your greatest opportunities

What always amazes me is that once you become aware and make a conscious choice as to who you want to be, life will always present you with an opportunity to demonstrate this aspect of who you are. Perhaps those opportunities are always present and we just never noticed them because we saw them as problems.

Most of us would choose a life that is problem free. A problem free life doesn't exist no matter how successful you are, or well balanced you are. Just remember that problems always present us with an opportunity to demonstrate who we want to be, and in overcoming these obstacles we change our core beliefs and many of the niggling, recurring issues we all experience from time to time either go away, or they don't bother us any more.

There were many times when I was really annoyed with myself for giving up a successful financial planning business. Finding myself in limbo after all my successes was one of the most awful phases I've been through. For a short while, I forgot I was powerful and acted like a victim (we all have a victim within us). I talked to everyone about my troubles and felt depressed and angry, but being a victim is not a very fulfilling role. It's true that you usually gain some attention in the short term but behaving like a victim doesn't change anything, and it doesn't make you feel any better about yourself. The problems that I experienced were just another opportunity for me to change some beliefs that had prevented me from creating the life I really wanted. The added bonus was that in helping myself, I am now able to help others.

If you want to end the patterns that keep recurring in your life and be successful—*you need to **be** first.*

Create a launching pad

It's difficult for anyone to demonstrate being something they are not when they feel as if they are at rock bottom. So, in order to get yourself to a point where you can work from, you do whatever you have to do to create a launching pad. A launching pad is a starting point, it's a place where you feel comfortable with yourself and with your situation.

When I experienced financial problems after my business failed I didn't feel powerful. If I'd tried to act it at that time I would have felt a fraud. This is the principle behind *fake it 'till you make it,* which is a superficial way of acting based on impressing others. Pretending may fool others but you can't fool yourself. When you act like the person that you want to be, for instance, responsible (or whatever the value is that you've chosen to demonstrate), you may not always feel confident to begin with. Over time this action becomes a natural way of responding and you create a new belief about what is possible for you. At that time you will feel confident and good about yourself. I needed to get myself to a point where I could support myself financially first, in other words to create a foundation before I could act confident and powerful.

As part of my second set of *being* values at that time I chose to be *honest* and *responsible*. I needed to be honest because I like to pay my debts and I also had to take responsibility for the situation that I created. I acted upon those values by obtaining part-time work so that I could pay my bills. I cannot describe how hard that was for me to do. Firstly, I was afraid when going for interviews that someone would have read my books and I'd be embarrassed for them to know I was working as a part-time bookkeeper. Secondly, I hadn't worked at that level for years and I wasn't sure I could understand the new computer systems, and thirdly I was used to being my own boss and doing things my own way. This option though was better for me than the alternative which was obtaining full-time work. I could have returned to a much better paying and more prestigious job as a financial planner, but that would have meant not being at home after school for Laura, and this was something I really wanted to do. It would also have taken time to re-establish a client base again and I preferred to use that time to create a business I loved, even though I didn't know what that was at that time. Although it felt painful, taking local part-time work was a short-term solution that allowed me to create a space where I could work out what I wanted and launch my dreams from.

By working part-time I had less time in a practical sense to work out what I wanted to do, however my experience has been that just thinking about what you want to do rarely provides solutions. When I stopped worrying about how to survive, and focused on acting on my values I became very clear about what was most important to me. I knew I wanted to help others and I started thinking about putting what I'd learned into a step-by-step formula. As I practised being honest and responsible I was asked to ghost write a book and from there my financial situation took a positive turn. Although to begin with I wasn't sure how I was going to use these steps the work I do today evolved from that point on.

When I talk about the Ten Steps, particularly *being* values, the one comment that I often receive is that I speak with conviction. That conviction has only come from living these steps myself because I know without any doubt that they work. We often try to run before we can walk and by doing this we actually hold ourselves back. Pretending won't get you to first base, being responsible and creating a launching pad will. There is no shame in having no money, being out of work, or having a marriage fail—they're not pleasant experiences but they are a part of life and there are opportunities within those situations for you. How you respond during tough times is what shapes your future.

You and your problems

Every problem, large or small, carries with it an opportunity for you to demonstrate who you want to be. If you are unsure of who you want to be, you need only look at the experiences of your everyday life for guidance. The patterns in your life are your opportunities.

When you accept what is and work on changing yourself rather than just your circumstances, the doors of opportunity will open automatically.

The following are some examples of the opportunities that problems present for you to think about:

- If you constantly experience money problems—you have an opportunity to be more responsible or creative.
- If you constantly have to prove that you are right—you have an opportunity to let go of your ego and practise being kind.
- If you are constantly criticised by others—you have an opportunity to be more independent and break free from the tribe.
- If nobody gives to you—you have an opportunity to be more generous to yourself.
- If you are unable to find work—you have an opportunity to be more self-reliant.
- If you experience conflict in relationships—you have an opportunity to value yourself more.
- If you experience constant health problems—you have an opportunity to be more honest about your real feelings.
- If you lurch from one crisis to another—you have an opportunity to accept responsibility for yourself.
- If you suffer from addictions of any kind—you have an opportunity to release your pain.
- If you feel unloved—you have an opportunity to be kind to yourself and others.

- When someone you love leaves or dies—you have an opportunity to grow.

Life is not always fair but it's always full of opportunities for you to choose who you want to be—that's what real positive thinking is all about.

A means to an end goal

Creating a launching pad is not to be confused with setting a means to an end goal. A means to an end goal is when you decide 'how' you'll achieve your goal, and the reason I don't favour this approach is because it can limit your opportunities.

Carol wanted to buy a 'Bed and Breakfast' establishment in the country. Although she had quite a large amount of money it wasn't enough to buy the type of property that she wanted. In order to be able to achieve her goal Carol decided that she had to obtain a job selling real estate that would pay high commissions. As she had no previous experience in this field this meant doing a training course first. Now to some people that may sound a very logical plan but the more I talked to Carol, the more apparent it became to me that she didn't really know what she wanted. This was the only solution she could think of.

Carol eventually acknowledged that in fact what she'd always wanted to do was to work as an interior decorator. However, she didn't feel other people would think she was good enough since she'd never completed a course in this subject. Although quite confident of her decorating abilities Carol had no idea where or how to start building this business. Once she gave herself permission to have what she really wanted and focused on being the person that she wanted to be, a number of opportunities opened up to her. Within months she bought a great home and was able to use this as a base for her business. She said to me, 'I just needed someone to believe in me'.

Now if Carol had followed her original plan she could have spent years doing work that she didn't really like only to find out when she achieved her goal that it wasn't what she really wanted. That's what people do all the time and it's a waste of time and money.

I'll go over this point again because some people find this concept hard to understand. A means to an end goal is where you decide how and when you will achieve your goals. This often involves a great investment of time and money, and because you believe there is only one way you limit opportunities. Creating a launching pad means that you take responsibility for where you are now and do whatever you need to do as a short term solution so that you can focus on creating what's really important to you.

Choosing, then living up to who you want to be, is your own personal code of honour—it's setting a standard of behaviour for yourself. Not only do your values provide you with guidelines for making decisions, they also present you with opportunities to change beliefs that no longer serve who you are, or what you want today. How you react to life's challenges that we all face is what will decide the quality of your life. You have total control over how much you allow into your life and total control over how much you contribute. Who you choose to be is your compass. Use it to guide all of your future choices and you will never make a wrong decision if you act on your highest values.

Step Three

Choose what makes you happy

You are constantly in the act of creating yourself. You are in every moment deciding who and what you are. You decide this largely through the choices you make regarding who and what you feel passionate about.
—Neale Donald Walsch

At one time or another most of us have made choices that were not wise or in our best interest. After repeated failures we tend to become more cautious, fearful of making more mistakes and we stop trusting ourselves. We caution others, and ourselves, to think things through, use our heads, weigh up the pros and cons, often thinking that if we had only thought things through more we would not be faced with some of the problems of today.

There are others though who say that you should choose not from your head but from your heart, so who is right?

Both are. Your heart is your compass and your head helps to bring your dreams to fulfillment. They work together.

When you make choices based solely on your intellect you may be successful and achieve all of your goals, but that is no guarantee you'll be happy with those choices. There are many rich, successful people who are unhappy. Choices made from the head are usually dictated by what other people think of you, or out of fear.

The key to living a happy, successful life is to know how to make the right choices, and there's a simple, effective way to do this. Ask yourself, 'What makes me happy?' This is not a question to ask just once. Ask yourself this question over and over again, over a period of at least a month or more. Write down all your answers. Carry a notebook with you and jot down every happy event and moment—no one incident is too small.

The following are some of the answers that one woman wrote to this question:

Spending time with my family and the people I care about
Paying my bills on time
Being valued
Doing work that is creative and personally fulfilling
Living in nice surroundings
A regular income
Working flexible hours
Having money to spend
Giving to others

Once you establish what makes you happy you can then relate each example of happiness to a value. For example, if you love to spend time in beautiful surroundings or love having a nice home, then beauty may be your value. If you like to pay your bills on time or to always have money available to you, then financial security may be your value. These are what I call your *having* values.

The *being* values are the character traits you choose to live by, whereas your *having* values are the material possessions and states that make you happy, and these are what you want to create more of.

When you've done this exercise, and it can take weeks (a coach can make this process easier by working with *having* values cards), you might notice that a pattern emerges where a particular value is repeated many times, you'll know that this rates highly with you.

You'll enjoy life more if you make this value a priority. Ultimately, your list will show you what your highest *having* values are. You'll see what I mean in the example shown below where financial freedom/security is mentioned three times, even though the goals may be different, the end result (which is the value) is always the same.

What makes me happy	***Value***
Spending time with my family and the people I care about	*Love*
Paying my bills on time	*Financial freedom*
Being valued	*Self-love*
Doing work that is creative and personally fulfilling	*Creativity/personal contribution*
Living in nice surroundings	*Beauty*
A regular income	*Financial security*
Working flexible hours	*Freedom*
Having money to spend	*Financial freedom*
Giving to others	*Generosity*

Being aware of what makes you happy and deciding on your *having* values in this manner will give you a far more accurate list of goals than one you could compile using just your intellect. Ask yourself often, 'What makes me happy?' and set your goals accordingly.

What you want is a feeling

I don't think there is a person alive who hasn't felt disappointed at some time and, often when we feel disappointed, we stop dreaming. We don't always get what we want, sometimes that's impossible but *we can always feel the way we want to feel.*

When we pursue a goal we are pursuing a feeling. When I wrote my first book I felt good about myself and enjoyed the recognition I received. Achieving these feelings were my real goal. I could have written a hit song, built a skyscraper, or won an a major sporting event and have achieved the same feeling. Someone who was once illiterate may get the same feeling from learning to read. If on the other hand, my book was published and no-one bought it then that feeling would have been short-lived and the joy of writing a book would diminish.

Sometimes what you want takes a while in coming, that doesn't mean that you'll never get it, and sometimes you don't get what you want, you get something far better.

I've never married, and whether I do or don't marry in the future is no longer an issue for me, but for many years finding the right man to share my life with was the most important goal in my life. If you'd told me at twenty five or thirty I would remain single I would have been devastated, and I'm glad I didn't know because I would have spent years of my life feeling unhappy about something unnecessarily. Although I didn't achieve that specific goal I am just as happy as if I had—because I achieved the feeling. I wanted love and companionship and I have them in my life in abundance. I feel blessed to have so much love in my life.

The tribe doesn't really believe that we can have everything that we want and often members of the tribe encourage us to put up with things the way they are—you don't have to. I was in a store one day when I heard the shop assistant, a woman about fifty, say, 'I can't wait to get old, then I can join some clubs and go out and have some fun'. What a waste of a lifetime.

If your life is not all that you want it to be choose again. There are many different ways to fulfil a need.

Add a dash of passion

Passion is what makes getting up in the morning fun, it makes your heart sing and it gives you the motivation to keep going when the going gets tough. Passion is your source of energy and anyone who thinks they're too old (or too young) for passion needs to think again.

Passion doesn't have to come from your work or a relationship, it can come from doing something for others. I read a letter in a Canadian magazine, *People and Possibilities*, that touched my heart. The letter was written by Tricia Crabtree about her daughter Taylor.

Tricia wrote that when Taylor was just seven years old she decided that she wanted to start her own business, she did this because she wanted to buy teddy bears and give them to children with cancer. She wanted sick children to, 'Have something special to hug and hug them back'. Taylor set a goal of giving away five hundred teddy bears and she started her own business selling hand painted hair clips to raise the money. As Taylor's business grew she encouraged other children to assist her. The following is an excerpt from Tricia Crabtree's letter:

The media picked up on Taylor's project and our community has embraced her efforts. But help has come from beyond our little community. Taylor has received donations from strangers that live thousand of miles away, just from word of mouth. It has been rather like a chain letter from the heart. With her scribbly second grade handwriting, she wrote each person with her appreciation and an update on her project. She has also expanded her project to include over one hundred other children (including special needs kids) as helpers. Taylor wanted other kids to feel that they too were capable of helping others in their own way. Along the way she (Taylor) raised her goal to seven hundred teddy bears.

Each day after selling, Taylor and her helpers talk about the people who have touched their hearts. Maybe it was the homeless man that donated eleven cents and was surprised when he was told that was plenty of money to buy a hair clip. He and Taylor stood together choosing just the right hair clip for his lady friend. Or maybe it was the young woman who was flying back home the next day to say goodbye to her father who was dying from cancer. Perhaps it was the man who drove all the way to his bank and back in order to buy a hair clip for his mum. He said that his dad had recently died from can-

cer. He wanted a child to have a teddy bear in his dad's memory.

With each hair clip or donation has come so many memories and a realisation that when working toward a goal from the heart, the journey too is part of the experience.

To date Taylor has given away thousands of teddy bears and her passion continues to touch the lives of many.

Passion is what transforms an ordinary life into something special.

Passions change as you change. I was passionate about financial planning for so many years, now it doesn't interest me at all and I don't even enjoy reading the financial pages any more. I think the passion came more from the recognition I received from that role which was exciting. There are so many things in my life that I'm passionate about at work, and in my leisure time, and they will continue to grow and change as I do.

Give yourself permission to have what you want

I always stress the importance of focusing on being the person you want to be—that's not to say there is anything wrong with wanting. Sometimes we can feel guilty for wanting so much, as if wanting more implies that we are not grateful for what we have. I believe that we have our dreams for a very good reason. Those dreams are what help us to learn and grow and ultimately to express love to others. My philosophy is very simple, if you have a dream then you have it for a reason, that means that you are entitled to have it manifest in your life and age for example, should not be a barrier.

Many of my clients are single women aged between thirty five and fifty five, and some of them would like to have a happy marriage but believe they are too old. One woman commented that she was proud of herself for being sensible because she'd finally settled for someone because he was a good man and she'd learned to love him. She later admitted there was no romance between them and she'd never really been in love.

I never encourage anyone to settle for less than they want because I don't think it's fair to yourself, and it's certainly isn't fair to the other person. However, if you are already in this type of relationship you don't have to leave your partner for things to change. You can change the relationship if you choose. If you want love and passion then make it a goal, but also be open to it coming in a different form to what you might have imagined.

When you are choosing what you makes you happy, remember to include every area of your life, that includes health and physical appearance, work, relationships and the lifestyle that you want. The key to living a happy life is balance.

When you don't know what you want don't rule out something because it seems too ordinary. Not all dreams have to be grand and some ordinary dreams may hold the key to a new opportunity.

When you don't know what you want

Confusion about what you want can occur when you've tried to achieve a goal before and failed. Or, you may believe that you can't have what you really want so you've buried the dream way down deep inside of you. Or, you may believe that you aren't good enough therefore you don't even acknowledge what you really want to yourself.

Remember this, *we always know what we want.* I've found that if you let people talk long enough they will tell you what that is. So many times a client has said to me, 'I don't know what I want', then a few minutes later they've very told clearly me what they want and haven't even realised it. When I point it out to them they usually say, 'Oh that!'.

If you don't know what work you want to do, ask yourself what needs do you want your work to fill. Do you want to feel stimulation and recognition, companionship or space to be alone? Do you want financial security or the opportunity to make a fortune? Do you want regular hours or a more flexible situation? Your feelings are your compass—don't ignore them.

A client once said to me, 'But what if I am not meant to have the things that I want? Maybe I'm meant to be a street sweeper, to struggle, maybe that's part of my life purpose'. I don't believe that any of us are born to do a specific thing—your life's purpose is about *being*.

What all our lives are about is demonstrating, through our daily actions, being the highest and best of who we are, so if you think that you can do that best by being a street sweeper and you enjoy it, go ahead. But if you want more from you life then that's equally okay.

Think of it this way. Would the world have been a better place if I had accepted that being a single mother meant I would struggle all my life? Some would say that was my karma. You create karma by what you choose to believe. By seeking the answers to my questions and choosing more for myself I have not only made my own life richer, I can share what I've learned with others.

Your life is a consequence of what you have chosen for yourself by your thoughts, words and how you've responded to life's event. If you don't love your life then you may find that difficult to accept, but I urge you to consider the possibility for therein lies your freedom. If your life is not all that you would consciously choose, then many of those choices have been made unconsciously, and no doubt have been influenced by tribal consciousness. Remember, the tribe believes in limitation. You have the power to transform your life in an instant and you can do more for yourself and others by being happy.

When you don't have a successful track record of setting and achieving goals, choose just one area of your life to work on at a time. It's possible to transform your entire life but if you take on too much too soon, the changes may be so far outside your comfort zone that you may begin to sabotage yourself. Begin by making small changes and as you do so you'll build a history of success, you can then use this foundation to build on to tackle the larger goals.

Remember when you pursue a goal, you are always pursuing a *feeling*. So, you can discover what you want simply by asking yourself how you want to feel. Spend your time thinking about and observing all that makes you happy, make a note of it by writing it down. Then choose it for yourself.

There's a difference between wanting and choosing

I want to make the distinction here between wanting and choosing. When you want something it's always outside of you and what is outside of you is hard to create. Every time you say 'I want' you reinforce the belief that you don't have it yet. When you choose something you claim it as yours. So, next time you are driving along in your car by yourself, try saying out loud all that you choose for yourself. I can guarantee you that you'll arrive at your destination feeling recharged. Choose what makes you happy today.

Setting goals

Once you choose what you want then you usually need to do something to manifest that desire. Some people like to set goals in a very linear fashion. They write their goals down, make a plan and set a date for their achievement, this is the traditional method for goal setting. But that method doesn't suit everyone.

When I worked as a financial planner I loved meeting, talking and helping my clients achieve their goals. I disliked writing the financial plan, that meant that sometimes I'd procrastinate as long as possible, often leaving it until the last minute to prepare the plan. I now believe procrastination is just a sign that you don't like what you're doing. I loved many aspects of being a financial planner but I also had mixed feelings about it as well. I now understand that was because the traditional financial planning way is contrary to my nature because it's about structured planning.

I am all for setting goals, I just don't like planning to achieve them in a structured way. If I make a plan that includes things that I should do by a certain date I feel oppressed, and when I feel oppressed I procrastinate, because I don't want to live that way. I need freedom and I get that when I have an *intention*.

The way I achieve goals is to meditate on what I want, give thanks in advance and I visualise myself as having achieved whatever it is that I desire. I only act when I feel intuitively led to do so. More than ever these days my life evolves at a faster rate. When I went into life coaching my intention was to help as many people as possible who felt lost like I'd once felt, to create a better life. I made a commitment to myself that I would do this even if it meant that I had to continue working as a part-time bookkeeper in order to make a living. I began training others to be life coaches as a result of a few people asking me to do so, and my business has just evolved from that point.

If you like to plan, that approach is equally valid for you. The point I want to emphasise is that one way is not better than another. There will be always people who will tell you that you have to do things in a certain way. Remember, they are only telling you about their rules. Honouring yourself is understanding your own personality and needs, and living a life that will fulfil those needs.

Step Four

You create your life with your thoughts, words and actions

Life is a creation not a discovery.
—Neale Donald Walsch

If you were to hold a magnet in one hand and a needle in the other and slowly move your hands together, the magnet would attract the needle and hold it to itself. The needle is powerless to change its destiny because its energy is scattered. However, if you were to realign the energy of the needle by stroking it with the magnet twenty or thirty times in one direction, the needle would become a magnet as well.

You and I are much like that needle. We have tremendous power to create anything that we desire but only when we learn to use our energy efficiently. Sadly the reality for most people is that they use their energy to create what they don't want. They do this by doubting themselves, dwelling on what they don't want, talking about problems and thinking negatively.

Our thoughts, words and actions are the energy source that we use to create what we want, or don't want. When you think constantly about what you don't want you will attract it, just as you attract what you do want when you think about it without worrying.

Successful people, ones who achieve their goals easily and effortlessly, use their energy efficiently. They think and talk positively about what they want and by doing so they attract people and opportunities into their life to help them manifest their dreams. This is called synchronicity.

Synchronicity is a term coined by Carl Jung which describes the power we all have to create our own coincidences. Coincidences don't just happen. They result from the energy field that we create with our thoughts, words and actions. In this step I have focused predominantly on thoughts and words, as actions, which are equally important, are covered in depth in Step Seven.

Synchronicity is something that I've experienced often but only when I don't scatter my energy by getting caught up in my intellect trying to work out 'how' I'm going to achieve my goals. When you dwell on 'how' you can achieve your goals you can also limit your opportunities. It's also very easy when you think about something too much to worry needlessly.

I mentioned earlier that when my son Robbie died I broke up with my business partner just a few weeks later; this left me with very little money at a very difficult time in my life. Not knowing what else to do I decided to start another secretarial service so that I would have a source of income. My focus was directed towards getting through each minute so I didn't worry about how I would find the money to start this business, I simply acted in complete faith that the means to create this business would come—and it did.

This was one of the few occasions when I went into something new with a complete absence of fear. As my focus was on what I wanted to create, and not on what could go wrong, I was able to attract to myself everything that I needed.

At the time of signing the lease for shop front premises I had only one month's rent behind me. Under normal circumstances I would have been very concerned about not having more money as security. This time it never occurred to me that I wouldn't find the money—I experienced no doubt, which is one of the Ten Steps. My dad, quite naturally, was concerned. Horrified is probably a better way to describe how he felt. When he learnt that I had signed a lease he said, 'Anne, how could you do it? How are you going to pay the rent on your house and an office when you don't know how much money you'll make?'.

I told Dad not to worry as I planned to sub-let the back office, an area that I wasn't using. Dad wasn't convinced that this would work and he pointed out, quite rightly, that the offices weren't very appealing; there was no floor covering in that area only concrete, no partitions or furniture, in fact nothing to appeal to a prospective tenant. These were all very valid concerns but they didn't concern me because I just *knew* the right person would come along. Remember, at that time all my energy was directed towards recovering from the trauma of my son's death, and because of this I didn't even think to question my intuition.

The following Saturday I acted on an impulse and looked in the Herald newspaper. This was the first time I had looked in the *Wanted to Rent* section. Listed that day was an advertisement from a Melbourne company looking for a Sydney office to share space with in our area. They also wanted someone intelligent to answer their phone and take orders. I rang and talked to Charles, their Sydney manager. We met, liked each other and his company agreed to sub-let the back office. The lease was signed within a week. Charles put up partitions and had floor covering laid. The rent they offered, which included payment for answering their phone and taking orders, was double the rent I paid for the entire office. They also paid additionally for the use of my photocopier, typing and they generously supplied all our tea and coffee. The arrangement was a very happy and harmonious one for both of us.

Months later I asked Charles what had prompted him to place the advertisement that weekend. He told me that he thought the whole idea to be ridiculous and said that he didn't believe they would ever find the right place or person to fit their criteria, however, the matter was taken out of his hands when his boss insisted that he place the advertisement. Some will always put this good fortune down to luck or coincidence. I know it was synchronicity. It doesn't matter how often it happens, I'm always in awe of the process. At some level we are all inter-connected, and our minds communicate.

I achieved my goal of creating an income at that time. With the value of hindsight I realise that I reacted, and understandably so, to the circumstances of my life, without thinking about what made me happy. As a result the business was successful but I didn't enjoy it, and as a consequence I sold it twenty months later.

There are no new ideas, just different ways of saying the same thing. The ideas contained in this book have been around for a long time. I may present them in a way that appeals to you so that they appear new, or maybe you've heard them before but weren't ready to act on them at that time. The point I want to emphasise is that all thought is creative and we create our world and our opportunities with our thoughts, words and actions.

We have been raised in a rational world where we are taught to believe only what we can see. It is understandable therefore that for some people accepting our thoughts and subsequently words and actions, can create our reality may seem hard to believe. Think of it this way, when we have a boom or a bust cycle it is always the result of a large group of people thinking and then acting in the same way, thus creating mass consciousness. In a boom market mass consciousness is optimistic and in a down cycle it's fearful.

When you follow the herd you give your power away to the tribe, and allow the masses to decide what you can do and have.

Think about how most people act when interest rates increase and the economy goes into a recessionary phase—a lot of people become fearful. They become afraid that there is not enough money for everyone and they worry about their job security and how they will survive. These are very real concerns if you believe you are powerless. But you don't have to be powerless, you can control your circumstances by thinking, talking and acting as if you have everything that you want. I've always found it interesting that the same amount of money is still in circulation during recessionary periods as boom cycle, it just changes hands. Ultimately the ones who prosper during these times are the ones who control their thoughts, words and actions.

Understanding invisible energy

This morning I opened my car door from inside my house. Some unseen force travelled fifteen metres from where I was standing, penetrated a double brick wall and unlocked my car doors—I have no idea how this energy force works, but I know it does because I see invisible energy at work everyday. Our world is dominated by invisible energy; the computer that I'm writing this book on, the Internet that allows me to communicate instantly with someone on the other side of the world, my mobile phone and microwave are all controlled by a force I cannot see, nor understand. Why then is it difficult to believe that we too are a source of invisible energy, that we constantly influence the world around us with our thoughts, words and actions?

Have you ever walked into a room and noticed that the atmosphere was tense? Most of us have experienced this at one time or another. If you have ever visited friends who have just had an argument you'll know what I mean—the tension is almost visible and so we say, 'You could cut the air with a knife'. This energy is mind energy. It can be a single energy or the collective energy of a group. You know when the atmosphere is festive simply by walking into a room, just as you know when the energy is sad. No-one usually has to say a word because you pick up on the emotions.

Some people are so powerful that they change the energy level in a room just by walking into it. Robert Schuller, an American minister and author is one of those people. Many years ago I attended one of his talks and I can still remember feeling the energy that emanated from him, even though I was a considerable distance away. I attended another seminar at which Louise Hay was speaking and from the moment Louise walked onto the stage the atmosphere in the conference hall changed. The feeling was great to begin with however, Louise's energy took us to a higher level. For the first few moments on stage Louise didn't even say a word, she just raised her arms in the air and the most incredible feeling of love radiated from her, it was almost tangible. Tony Robbins is another speaker who has incredible presence. He exudes power, confidence and energy.

Betty Shine in her book, *Mind Waves*[2], says:

> *'When someone is angry, their mind energy expands, as anger is a very positive state of mind. As it expands it causes waves of energy rather like shock waves and it's these vibrations that one can feel. The same thing applies to a person who is excited. There would be an aura of excitement around them. If a person is miserable, then their mind energy would be drawn in, absorbing energy from those around them rather like a vampire sucking blood. That is why one feels exhausted in the company of these people. Being with someone who is depressed can actually cause depression in others.'*

As our emotions, like waves of energy, flow from us, we attract to ourselves people who are on the same frequency as we are—much like a radio receiver. If, for instance you are feeling optimistic and joyful you'll radiate and attract other happy people to you. On the other hand, if you're a pessimist and believe that nothing ever goes right, you'll attract others to yourself with a similar viewpoint.

It's not that we don't meet people on different wavelengths everyday, we do. But the people that we'll be attracted to, the job we choose or the friends that we spend time with for example, will be on the same mind wave frequency a fair amount of the time. That's why sometimes we outgrow people, because as we grow and learn more about ourselves, and take control of our thoughts and words we switch to a different frequency and as a result we find that we have nothing in common with our old friends any longer.

Think about a time when you felt down in the dumps. Maybe you had a bad day at work, or you were short of money. Who did you meet or talk to when you felt that way? Think again about a time when you felt fantastic. Who did you socialise with then? Have you ever found that you talk to certain people when you feel down and other people when you feel good? Most of us do, and that's because we are drawn to people on the same energy level at a given moment.

When I was struggling with money and unhappy about the work I was doing I had one very good friend that I would ring every week. She, in turn would talk about her money worries and we would try to work out solutions. When I became aware that this wasn't a positive habit, I stopped talking about my problems to her—and discovered that we had nothing in common. We still like each other and I still consider her a friend but now we talk about once a year.

When you begin to understand how powerful your thoughts and words are, and what impact they have on your daily life, you will begin to think twice before you allow yourself to dwell on what you don't want for long.

Think about what you're creating in your life right now. Are you drawing to you people and experiences that you want to have? Or, are you attracting experiences that you would prefer not to have?

Betty Shine suggests this exercise[2]. Choose a peaceful room in your home and sit quietly for ten minutes. Allow your mind to go blank and just absorb the atmosphere allowing yourself to become a part of it. As you are drawn into this atmosphere become aware of the waves of energy that surround you. This will give you a good idea of the atmosphere in your home. If you don't like it you can change it by laughing, meditating, or simply doing things that make you happy in your home. You could do the same at work or in any situation that doesn't suit you.

Your creative tools

The tools that you create with, moment by moment, day by day, are your thoughts, words and actions. Bill Gates, one of the richest man in the world, uses the same tools to create wealth as the man who sleeps on a park bench uses to create poverty. Moment by moment you choose what you wish to create and experience. You can use these tools wisely or you can squander them and live your life by accident.

I was once challenged on this point by a woman I met at a talk I was giving. She commented, 'I cannot accept that I created an abusive husband'. Without knowing her history I can't comment on what her thoughts and beliefs were to attract such a person into her life. I do know however that we always have power over how we respond and what we allow to stay in our lives. I suggested to the woman that perhaps she had played her role in creating this situation because she allowed the abuse to continue. After some consideration she did agree that this was the case.

At one stage I had a boss who often made very cutting remarks and could be extremely rude. He would regularly pick on one person and belittle them during our regular training sessions. I would often sit during those sessions and think that he wouldn't like to talk to me that way because I simply wouldn't tolerate it. There were occasions when he would look at me and I would feel as if he was going to say something, but he never did. This is because he knew instinctively that I was someone he couldn't push around.

You may have met people who appear to be incredibly negative, yet they still seem to succeed. I must admit that for many years I couldn't quite understand how this could be. Over time I came to understand how this happens.

Steve once owned a very successful construction business. However, he began to experience financial difficulties when his business partner was unable to meet his financial commitment in a major development. Steve managed to hold on to the business for a couple of years, paying both his and his partner's share of the interest payments until eventually he was forced to close the business down. By selling his home and all his assets he just managed to avoid bankruptcy.

He moved interstate and started over again, living in a one bedroom flat and doing work that he'd once done as an apprentice builder. Without spending a cent on advertising he obtained building work from word-of-mouth recommendations. During his first year he made only an average income. However, by the second year his new business turned over a million dollars. It was around this time Steve was approached by a lawyer who wanted him to participate in a development which was low risk and looked likely to be very profitable. Within three years Steve was making more money than he had ever made from his former business.

Steve was one of the people I worked for as a bookkeeper during the period when I worked part-time and I had the opportunity to observe him over several months. Steve was a born worrier and often talked negatively and this confused me for at first. After awhile I became aware that Steve's core belief was that he was an above average builder, which he was, and that he was a good businessman. Even though he worried and sometimes talked negatively, most of the time he dwelled on the opportunities he created and how to maximise them. Despite this I couldn't help but wonder just how much more successful Steve could be if he hadn't scattered his energy by worrying and talking negatively.

Our core beliefs play a major role in the life we create. These act like the foundations for our life. Our thoughts, words and actions create the structure. How solid and easy that structure is for you to create is decided on a daily basis by how you think, speak and act.

Real power and enormous success manifests when your thoughts, words and actions totally support each other. Each one of these is a powerful source of energy and each one vibrates on a different energy level. For instance, if you think positively and speak negatively you'll attract some of what you want, but never enough. If you think and speak positively but fail to act, you'll attract even more but not as much as is possible. However, when your thoughts, words and actions are totally in alignment, you become magnetic and your potential is unlimited.

The law of cause and effect

Every thought you have, and every word that you say about another, goes out into the universe and ricochets back to you. If you gossip and criticise another then this will come back to you in some form. The other person may never know what you've said, but you are the one that will suffer the consequences from the negative energy that you put out.

If you have constant problems in your life—even simple everyday ones such as tradespeople not turning up when they promise—and you talk about it to everyone you meet, you are actually using your energy to create more of the same.

Experts tell us that between thirty thousand and sixty thousand thoughts circulate in our minds each day. Out of sixty thousand thoughts you have during one day how many do you imagine supports the life that you want to create for yourself? And how many of those thoughts do you use to create what you don't want?

Think about your thoughts

The thoughts that circulate in your mind dictate how you feel. Let's say you are thinking about things that you love and enjoy, then you're going to feel happy. On the other hand if you are worrying about how you'll pay the bills on time you'll most likely feel anxious or depressed. How you feel in turn influences the decisions and choices that you make. The cycle goes like this:

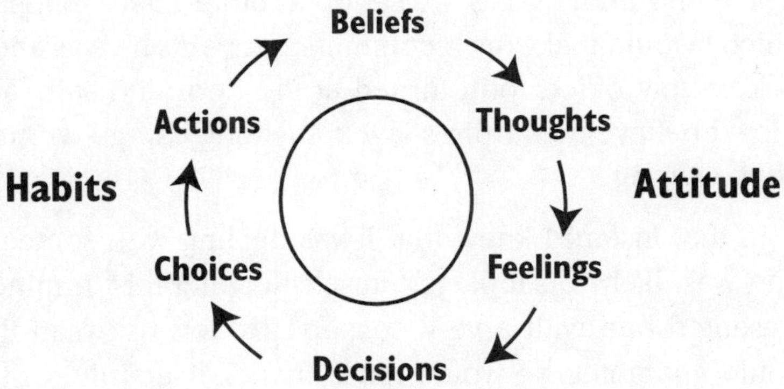

What you think about influences how you'll feel, and how you feel in turn influences all of the decisions, choices and actions that you make.

The good news is that you don't have to be a victim of your thoughts—you have the power to choose what thoughts circulate in your mind. It's only natural that you'll experience negative or fearful thoughts at times, we all do. Your power lies in the choices that you make. You can allow your mind to dwell on whatever pops into your consciousness. Or, you can choose to cancel worrying or fearful thoughts as soon as you become aware of them and replace them with thoughts that will help you create the life you really want.

When I was working as a financial planner a man, aged about sixty (I'll call him John) consulted me for advice on how to invest his superannuation payout. On retirement he would receive a considerable sum of money, which was more than he had ever had in his life. The sum was large enough to ensure that he would never have to worry about money again. After the usual discussion to assess his risk profile and future goals, we set up another appointment at which I would make my recommendations. As he was about to leave my office John turned at the door and said, 'You know, I believe in Murphy's law. If anything can go wrong it will go wrong'.

In that instant I knew that I was dealing with someone who was likely to sabotage himself. Keeping this in mind, I presented him with a very conservative low-risk plan that would guarantee he would have financial security for the rest of his life. However, at our next meeting he rejected my recommendations, although he wanted me to continue as his adviser. He chose to invest in high risk, high return investments in order to increase his capital. At that time we were experiencing a boom market and at first his investments rose in value. Six months later his marriage broke up and his wife remained in the family home. He cashed in half of his investments to finalise their property settlement. Even so, he still had a reasonable sum to live comfortably on for the rest of his life. Only a few months later the stock market crashed and his investments along with it. Instead of enjoying a comfortable retirement, this man ended up living in a one bedroom unit and was dependent on the old age pension. His belief in Murphy's law created his reality.

We can't control what pops into our mind, but we can control what we choose to dwell on. As you consciously choose to think about the things that you desire in your life, you will find that all of your thoughts will, over time, follow suit. Your mind is not a separate part of you that you have no control over, your mind simply responds to the messages that have been fed into it, by yourself and the tribe, over your lifetime.

A friend once asked me to seal a terracotta pot for her and I agreed to do so. When it was dry, I placed the pot onto the passenger seat of my car as I planned to deliver it back to her. As I drove up the road from my house the pot rolled onto the floor, and my first reaction was to save it. I automatically reached out to grab the pot, which was on my left, and as I did so I turned the car wheel to the left without thinking and hit a series of posts that lined the side of the road. By trying to save a $20 pot I had to pay $300 excess on my car insurance to have the car repaired.

I didn't consciously choose to hit those posts but I did forget momentarily a most important point—*what you focus your energy on you attract*. I focused on what was to the left of me and not on what was ahead. That's what we do all the time when we think about things that we don't want to happen.

As you read this you may be tempted to think, 'I know all this' however, having an understanding at an intellectual level and putting it into action every single day are two very different things. You need to remember that you can't afford the luxury of fearful thinking because it infiltrates every cell in your body. Louise Samways author of, *Your MindBody Energy*[3], says, 'Our conscious awareness of the material world is located in our heads, whereas our 'mind' in located throughout our body'.

The mind body connection

Psychologist, Paul Pearsall confirms Louise Samways' belief that memory is stored in every cell of the body in his book, The Heart's Code[4]. Paul Pearsall tells many stories of transplant patients who, after receiving donor hearts, have memories and tastes that belong to their donors.

In one story he tells of a couple who were driving home after dining out. While driving along in their car they engaged in an argument. Their car crashed killing the husband. Two years later the distraught wife met with the recipient of her husband's heart, a non-English speaking Spanish boy. As she put her hand over the boy's heart she asked her husband for forgiveness, repeating the word her husband and she had invented to symbolise the end of a fight. That word was 'copathetic'. The boy asked what 'copathetic' meant, as he'd been saying it for two years.

Change the way you act

Everyone experiences negative and fearful thoughts at times. The choice that you have is whether you allow yourself to dwell on these thoughts or not. There is nothing wrong with getting angry, hurt, depressed and so on and I am not for one moment suggesting that you suppress your feelings, or that you never talk about how you feel. Acknowledge your feelings by all means and do whatever you need to do to release them, just don't get stuck in your feelings. Remember that your thoughts impact on your words, and ultimately your actions, in turn taking you away from a life you love.

Let me give you an example of how easily we can allow ourselves to be sidetracked by everyday issues. Imagine you had a bad day at work, the boss unjustly accused you of doing something that you didn't do and you come home from work understandably upset. You begin the evening by telling your partner about the bad day that you had at work. That night you get on the telephone to a friend and tell them about your bad day. The next day you return to work and talk to your co-workers about the unfairness of the situation, or how much you dislike your job. Now, this behaviour is what keeps you stuck in your emotions because each time you think about the situation you recreate the event by focusing more emotion on it. A better way to handle the situation would be to talk about what happened once, do something to release the anger like exercise, meditation or writing in a journal, then let it go. That way you are more likely to have positive discussions with your friends and feel uplifted as a result, rather than reliving yesterday's problems.

I've sometimes found that when I remind a client to let go of negative thoughts they may become defensive and say something like, 'Well of course I've let it go, it doesn't bother me any more'. Clearly indicating an issue for them if they're still talking about it. If you want your life to really work you need to stop deluding yourself and become aware of your own self-defeating behaviour. This is not a judgement about you, it's probably just a habit, but until you can recognise self-defeating behaviour—you can't change it.

The power of words

At one time I was standing in line hoping to buy Seinfeld tickets for my daughter when a woman started talking to me. Our queue was alongside the electrical goods department in a major department store and big screen TVs were playing—she sighed as she said, 'Wouldn't you love a TV like that?'. Before I had a chance to reply she started talking about the man who used to live next door to her who has a big screen TV. She went into great detail telling me about this man, what work he does, and how much money he makes and how beautiful his home is. Finally she drew breath and said, 'Who would want to be rich anyway—it doesn't make you happy'.

Have you noticed this is what people do everyday? They envy others then at the same time attempt to justify why they can't have what they want. I couldn't help myself from saying, 'Having things that you want doesn't make you unhappy either'. Taken aback she quickly changed the subject.

Words are a precious gift that we often carelessly squander. You may be limiting yourself by going along with the crowd and talking like everyone else, or by always agreeing with them.

Choose your words carefully. Every time you say something like, 'I can't believe it', 'It's too good to be true', 'You can't win', 'If it's not one thing, it's another', or 'That's just my luck' you are actually using your energy to make these statements true for you. Equally, when you constantly talk about wanting something, you are effectively expressing the belief that you can't have it.

Saying 'I want' is a term that states that you don't have it yet. As long as you keep saying 'I want', you won't get it. Change your words to 'I am', 'I have' or 'I choose' and you change the energy completely. Words are incredibly powerful. The difference between saying 'I want to succeed' and 'I am successful' is enormous, and such affirmations are used by athletes and peak performers in all areas of life.

Using positive affirmations means that you say you have something *before* it shows up in your life. The reason you do this is because your subconscious doesn't know the difference between fact and fiction. So in order to create the life you want you need to speak and act as if you already have your desires. By doing this you use your energy to attract opportunities to you that will help you manifest those desires.

Positive affirmations help you to stay focused. Suze Orman, author of *The Nine Steps to Financial Freedom*, calls affirmations 'statements of truth'. I like that phrase as a statement of truth sounds more powerful than an 'affirmation'. However, it doesn't really matter what you call them providing you understand the concept and use it to assist you in creating a life you love.

Affirmations have become statements of truth for me. When I wanted to buy a home I discovered that all the areas where I wanted to live were out of my financial reach. I would constantly juggle figures trying to work out ways to achieve my goal of living in one of my preferred areas. Once I stopped trying to work out 'how' I could achieve this goal and affirmed, 'I am a home owner', the perfect opportunity came my way the next day and I moved into my home four weeks later. Although my home isn't in an area as prestigious as my first choice, it did match every requirement on my list. The area I live in is a place that I now prefer to my original first choice because of its close proximity to the ocean and the relaxed life style.

Some people say they can't say affirmations because they feel they are lying, I don't consider it lying to state something in advance. I know it's going to happen. However, if this is the case for you, you can turn your statements into questions.

The power of questions

If you have a habit of saying, 'I can't afford it', say instead, 'How can I afford it?' By turning the statement into a question, you create an entirely different perspective on a situation and open up a whole new set of possibilities.

When you ask a question you give yourself permission to have what you really desire—and this opens many doors. When the doors open, you may then find that you don't want whatever it is enough, or you aren't prepared to make the commitment to achieve that desire which is an entirely different situation.

Not far from where I live there are a number of 'battle axe' blocks overlooking the lake and ocean. As these houses aren't visible from the road I wondered for a long time what they are like. One Saturday I saw an advertisement for one of these properties listed for sale and I took the opportunity to take a look when it was open for inspection. I fell in love with the house that was for sale. I came home feeling depressed because the house was out of my price range and knowing that these houses rarely come onto the market, I felt like I was missing out on a golden opportunity. So I asked myself, 'How can I afford it?' and I remained open to the possibility of buying it. The next week I went back and looked at the house again, only this time from the perspective of a prospective purchaser and I viewed the home with entirely different eyes. Although the house was beautiful and the location outstanding, I decided the house wasn't my dream home after all as it didn't have everything I wanted. This time I was able to walk away knowing that this particular house wasn't right for me.

Now this result may not always be the case, however by turning a statement into a question you may open up a way that you've never thought of before.

The important thing is to become aware of the statements that you make regularly. You may find that you limit your work opportunities by saying you're too old, over-qualified or under-qualified. Or, you may limit the salary you receive by saying your employer can't or won't pay you any more. Think about the statements you most commonly say and turn them into questions, and there's a good chance that you'll find a way to get what you want—a way that may never have occurred to you while you were so busy telling yourself you couldn't have it, do it, or be it.

Questions can lead you to solutions, open up opportunities and help you start the day on the right footing. Each day I begin and end my meditation with the question, 'How can I live my life today to my fullest potential, for myself and all mankind?'. That question helps me to stay focused on what's most important to me.

I suggest that you don't leave it another day to review your vocabulary; it really influences every aspect of your life.

Here are some words and expressions you can use to replace the ones that no longer support the life you want. Add your own as well.

Cancel these words	**Suggested replacement**
I can't....	*How can I....?*
It's hard	*It's a challenge*
problem	*opportunity*
by myself	*with myself*
struggle	*working towards*
broke	*temporarily low on cash*
It's too good to be true	*Good things always happen to me*
going around in circles	*another opportunity*
It's no use	*It's my turn*
should	*could*
have to	*choose*
want	*I choose*
You can't win	*I always win*
I can't afford	*Choose not to*

Align your energy

Thoughts, words and actions all create on different energy levels. Life can be a lot easier when you align your thoughts, words and actions so you attract all that you desire. Remember, if you think and speak positively but don't act on opportunities, you may manifest some of what you desire but not all. Action is making a commitment to yourself; it's a visible way of demonstrating that you have no doubt.

Commitment means doing

Doubts and fears are natural however, it's useful to remember that they are only feelings—they have no power except that which you give them through your thoughts, words and actions.

It's not necessary to feel confident. You just do whatever is necessary to create what you want, the feeling follows later. Many people are happy to think positively and talk positively but when it comes to stepping out in faith, sometimes into an unknown abyss, they stop. You don't have to take unnecessary risks, you simply need to be prepared and be ready to act on opportunities when they come your way.

If you like planning but don't know how to actually start doing, think about what you really desire. What would make your heart sing? Now, imagine yourself as having already achieved that goal. Think about what you would have done to get to that place, then work backwards, taking one step at a time. Ask yourself what you did at each step along the way and you may find a way to begin right now.

If making plans is not your style, think about what you can do now. Can you visualise the outcome you desire? Can you affirm for it? Do you need to learn some more, develop a skill or do more research?

If the journey seems too hard it may be that you aren't committed enough yet, you simply don't want whatever it is enough, or you have some healing to do first. So go back, and take note of what makes you happy and remember that happiness and fulfillment are part of your life purpose; it's not just about the attainment of material possessions or goals.

Step Five

Face your fears

Experiences repeat themselves until they are learned.
—John Gray

Some people seem to experience recurring problems in relationships, it doesn't matter how many times they change partners, jobs, or friends, the same issues arise again and again. For other people money is the problem. They may have a tendency to overspend and run up debts, then they reorganise their finances vowing this will never happen again and before long they are back where they started, or in a worse position.

Recurring patterns are your signposts, and your opportunities, although they never feel like it at the time. If you have any type of recurring problem you have an opportunity to face your fears, by doing so you free yourself from having to experience the same situations over and over again.

It's tempting at these times to look at what's causing the problem externally, in other words to blame someone, or something else. This could be the Government, your employer, the economy, the people who lent you money or won't lend you money, or another person. If you're not blaming someone else you might be blaming yourself.

It doesn't matter whether you're right or wrong, the fact is that acting in this way won't change the situation nor will it help you create a life you love.

When you acknowledge that you have control over your life and you stop blaming other people or luck for the situation you're in, then you are ready to face your fears. When you do this you will find that you have one of three opportunities, sometimes you have all three rolled into one.

Opportunity One: Every problem presents you with an opportunity to demonstrate who you want to be; this demonstration allows you to change a limiting belief.

This point was covered in Step Two but I want to reinforce it at this time because it's so important.

Bronwyn's story

When I selected my second set of being values I decided I wanted to be powerful and started making plans to clear my debts so that I could buy a home of my own. Three weeks after I started working towards this goal my boss called me into his office on a Friday afternoon and asked me to resign. I was shocked and my first reaction was to refuse, which turned out to be a wise decision as my employer wouldn't have had to pay their contribution to my superannuation fund if I'd agreed.

So, I was sacked. A victim of corporate politics. I was asked to pack up my desk immediately and hand back the keys to the company car. I had worked for the company for seven years, there were no problems with my work, and I didn't see it coming. I was in a daze when I called a cab to take me home.

In the past I would normally have rung all my friends and talked about the injustice of the situation for weeks, I would have acted like a victim. This time I decided not to talk about it, and to lay low for awhile, lick my wounds and think about what I really wanted. I still found it hard to believe that I could have created this and at the time it was hard to see the opportunity in this situation.

After a few days I asked myself, 'How would a powerful person act in this situation?'. I realised that this could be an opportunity to start my own business as a public relations consultant. This was something that I'd always wanted to do, but I'd found it hard to give up the security of a well-paying job. Even though I felt extremely fearful I decided to follow my heart.

The first thing I did was to let everyone know that I was in business. I registered a business name and had business cards and letterheads designed and printed. I didn't need much money to get started. I already had a computer and could work from home, but I still needed cash flow to pay my rent and living expenses until the business was established.

I had a small amount of money in savings, plus my holiday pay. I calculated that if I lived frugally and supplemented this money with a small amount of regular income I could survive for six months, by which time the business should be able to support me. I took a part-time job cleaning offices, which meant I was able to work early in the morning and be home by 9a.m., so my days were free to work on building my own business.

Acting like a powerful person I also made a contingency plan, just in case I didn't generate sufficient income from my business in the time allowed. Fortunately I didn't need to put that plan into place, as twelve months after being sacked I was making three times my former salary.

I acted like the person that I wanted to be and as a result I now know that I can achieve anything I want.

Once you make a decision to act on who you want to be, life will always present you with an opportunity to demonstrate that aspect of yourself.

Opportunity Two: You are able to realise what emotional benefit you are gaining—the pay-off—from having your problems.

By pay-off, I mean the reward you get from keeping up a behaviour. Pay-offs can be subtle and not always easy to discover by yourself and that's because pay-offs often hide a deep-seated fear, or an erroneous belief.

So many people have said to me, 'Anne, I am ready to change' and they mean it on a conscious level. Then the next week they come back with all sorts of excuses as to why they haven't been able to take the steps they agreed upon at our last session. In most cases this resistance is only fear coming to the surface, sometimes it's easier to live with a situation you know, even if it's unpleasant, rather than risk the pain of facing a deep-seated fear. The expression, 'Better the devil you know than the devil you don't' sums up this situation.

Mary had an issue with money. She owned a small shop and her income fluctuated; it didn't matter how hard she worked, there was never enough money to meet all her obligations. During one session Mary made a comment about how happy she was in her marriage. As I knew this was her second marriage, I asked her if she'd experienced problems with money during her first marriage, a relationship that she'd told me was very unhappy. Mary thought for a moment and said that she and her first husband always had lots of money. Mary looked up with surprise, at that moment she became aware that she had unconsciously associated having money with pain, and having no money with happiness, it became apparent that whenever it looked like business was picking up and more money would come in, Mary would unconsciously sabotage herself.

Although we can often see what's holding others back I have learnt that individuals need to acknowledge their own pay-offs for themselves. If you try force someone to face their fears before they are ready you only create more resistance.

You may like to consider some examples of pay-offs below to see if any of them apply to you.

You get attention. Always having a problem to talk about can get you a lot of attention and sympathy. Try not talking about any problems in your life for at least two weeks and notice the difference it makes and how you feel.

If you feel neglected or lonely then you know you can choose a more positive way to gain the attention you desire.

If you can't think of any ways to do this then model the behaviour of someone you admire.

You take revenge. This is often the case in marriage breakdowns. For instance, a woman who continually struggles after a marriage breakdown can still exert control over her ex-husband by making him feel guilty. If she were to become financially independent there would be no payoff—and he would be 'off the hook'. I've also known men who've lost their jobs and been unemployed for long periods of time after an acrimonious break up. Unconsciously this was their way of getting back, or refusing to support a former partner. Whenever you want to make someone pay then you have not resolved your own feelings about that person.

If a teenager or adult rebels against parental expectations by doing work that is below his potential, or not working at all, he could be taking revenge against a controlling parent. While this behaviour may achieve the desired effect it obviously sabotages the person concerned because the long term consequences will far outweigh the benefit he temporarily gains.

The way to change both of these situations is by forgiving the other person and accepting responsibility for yourself.

Problems prevent you from facing the real issue. Symptoms such as being overweight or having money problems may appear to be what's holding you back, however they may also be providing you with a way out so that you don't have to face the real issue.

Often behind the issue is a fear is that you're not good enough, or a belief that you can't have what you really want.

By acting on your chosen *being* values you can change any limiting belief.

You're afraid of people discovering you're a fraud. A large percentage of the population lives with the fear of 'not being good enough'. Recurring problems can prevent you from pursuing what you really want so that you don't have to face these feelings of inadequacy.The solution again is to act on your *being* values.

You will do better than your family/friends. One of my clients became aware that she was holding herself back because she was afraid to do better than her husband, whose business was struggling. This awareness allowed her to face the real issues in her relationship honestly. Once she did this the relationship survived and her business flourished. The way to change this pay-off is to acknowledge what the real issue is and deal with it.

You're afraid of change. Most people fear change. Remember that living a life you love doesn't necessarily mean giving up the things that you enjoy. Often though you need to step into the abyss of the unknown before your life can change positively. It's possible to change this pay-off by keeping your focus on what you really want and off what you don't want.

Discovering your pay-off

Sometimes you'll read an example such as one of the above and you'll recognise instantly what your pay-off is. This is when you are ready to change. At other times the real reason eludes you. One way to become more aware is to ask yourself, during a quiet time or meditation, what your pay-off is. You may need to ask more than once. My experience has been that if you are open and patient awareness always comes. Then once you know what's holding you back, you can take whatever steps are necessary to change the belief and subsequently the pattern of behaviour. If you are unsure as to how to change, follow the same process of going within and ask your intuition for guidance on what changes to make.

Opportunity three. You can face some unresolved emotions that need to be dealt with.

Even when you discover what your pay-off is there is usually more work to be done. To get your life to really work, to leave pain and sadness behind, you need to allow yourself to feel.

During childhood, most of us were conditioned not to show anger or fear—we learnt that some feelings just aren't okay to have or show. The traditional role of parents was dictatorial. You might have heard an adult say to a child, 'Don't you get angry with me, just do as you're told' or 'Big boys don't cry'. Phrases such as this get passed down from one generation to another and we learn from them that some feelings just aren't okay. Remember that your parents may have had the best intentions but most times they have only taught you what they themselves had been taught. You know better now. To find real freedom you now need to reverse that conditioning and give yourself permission to feel all of your feelings.

Beware of getting stuck

Traditional psychology encourages talking about problems as a way of releasing emotion. This is a method that works for many, however some people become addicted to their problem because they confuse their problem with who they are. You sometimes hear people describe themselves as 'co-dependent' 'alcoholic' or as having an 'addictive personality'. Sometimes they become so attached to the label or to their story that they are not willing to let it go.

Caroline Myss in her book, *Why People Don't Heal and How They Can*[5], *says:*

> *Imagine, you are told, that every one of us carries within us a part that feels like a Victim. For some of us, our Victim surfaces whenever we are in an intimate relationship. For others, our Victim begins to speak every time we are asked for our opinion on something. For others still, our Victim is forever telling us ahead of time what to expect when we get 'there', no matter where 'there' is.*
>
> *Now you are asked, 'What if you were given the opportunity to face that part of yourself and rid yourself of that negative influence once and for all. Would you take it?*

It seems crazy to imagine that someone would want to remain a victim but it's a sad fact of life that many do. Being a victim is very rarely a conscious choice, however it's easy to become one by constantly talking about problems. Problems can be a way of gaining attention, love and support that some people wouldn't normally get (the pay-off). If it appears your problems are providing you with a source of love and attention then why would you want to give them up?

It's tempting for us all to trot out stories of traumatic events, abuse, betrayal, illness, financial loss or hardship of some kind. However, when we do this often enough we start to identify who we are with what has happened to us and as a consequence, over time we actually start thinking of ourselves as victims. Even though we may want to change the situation, we actually become bonded to that state.

You've probably met someone for whom telling their story has become an addiction. When you get tired of listening to them, they tend to move on, constantly seeking new audiences to give them attention or pity. Yet, the more they do this, the more they become bonded, or stuck in their past.

John Gray describes how some emotions take you around in circles and support you in remaining 'stuck', while other emotions allow you to heal. Some of John Gray's examples of these emotions are shown below.

Emotions that keep you bonded to your pain	***Emotions that allow you to heal***
Blame	*Anger*
Hate	
Resentment	
Anxiety	*Fear*
Self pity	
Guilt	*Sadness*
Doubt	
Depression	*Sorrow*
Hopelessness	
Helplessness	
Indifference	
Unworthiness	

Your objective is to go beyond emotions that keep you bonded to your pain. For instance, if you feel depressed or anxious, allowing yourself to dwell on these feelings changes nothing. However, if you ask yourself what's at the root of your depression you'll find sorrow or sadness; this is the emotion that you need to allow yourself to feel so that you can get on with your life. The same applies to anxiety: we all know that worrying doesn't change a thing. You can develop new habits that will break the worry cycle but usually underneath worry is a fear, and that's the emotion you need to acknowledge and feel in order to break the habit.

Choose to allow yourself to really feel emotions that will help you to heal, and by doing this you may also recognise a limiting belief that is preventing you from having what you really want. For instance, if you feel helpless or depressed, underneath these feelings is usually a belief that you can't have what you really want. If you feel resentful or unworthy you may have a core belief that you're not good enough. Remember, your feelings are your compass and even so called 'negative' feelings can serve their purpose if they help you to make positive changes.

What are you feeling at your core?

It may be anger, and perhaps you've never really allowed yourself to feel angry because that would mean feeling bad about yourself. Or, it may be sorrow, and you may not have realised that any loss needs to be grieved. You may have denied your sorrow and by doing so missed the opportunity to grieve so that you could then get on with your life.

By acknowledging the underlying emotions of fear, anger, sadness and sorrow you can experience what you really feel then you can let it go and the past will release its hold on you.

Garry Lynch, the father of murder victim Anita Cobby, once said to me,'You have to walk through the fire first'.You need to feel the pain before you can leave it behind.

The difficulty for most of us is in discovering what emotions are holding us back as we may have never acknowledged them. A major reason for this is that we have been taught to be 'nice' people and nice people often don't like to admit, even to themselves, that they are capable of feeling strong emotions such as anger or rage, particularly when those feelings are directed towards someone they love. In fact, the more intense the pain, the more expert you become at suppressing what you really feel—often to the point that you have no conscious knowledge of the pain's existence. For instance, my son died in front of my daughter Lisa, who was twelve years old at the time. Even though twenty years have passed Lisa has no conscious memory of that day, or even the months that followed—it's an experience she has totally blotted from her memory as the pain was so overwhelming. Although this is an extreme case it's what we do whenever we feel an emotion, or associated pain that's too difficult for us to acknowledge. Instead we hide our real feelings behind more seemingly manageable issues, which may irk us on a day to day level, but are unlikely to rock our very foundations. However, even though your conscious mind denies the existence of it, the pain still affects you.

There is no way to avoid pain, the only way to move past it, is to walk through it. You can delay facing pain until you are stronger but you can't put it off forever. The longer you try to avoid it, it will continue to follow you around and eventually it will control your entire life.

Give yourself permission to feel

The answer to everything lies within. When you are open and willing to allow any suppressed emotions to surface, and you give yourself permission to feel, you may notice a crack appearing in the façade that you present to yourself and the world. If you're willing you'll soon discover what's holding you back. However, if you feel that you need help through this time I suggest you seek assistance from a qualified professional, such as a counsellor or a therapist.

The pain I felt when my son died was beyond anything I can describe. There were times when I had to shut out the pain because I felt I wouldn't survive the intensity of it. However, because the pain was so bad and I just wanted it to end I had the motivation to feel it so that I could move beyond it. I couldn't imagine anything worse than carrying that agony around with me for the rest of my life. Today I can talk about my son in the same manner as I talk about my girls. There is rarely any sadness attached to his memory, I only think lovingly of him. I love him, the happy memory of him is a part of my life, it's that aspect I choose to hold on to rather than the memory of the pain associated with his death. I am just so grateful for the time that we shared.

However, what had a more detrimental effect on my daily life over the longer term were the emotions that I didn't deal with associated with being a single parent, and the rejection and abandonment that was a part of my life for so long. It was during menopause that these emotions surfaced.

I have noticed that as women enter menopause it's not uncommon for repressed anger to surface—it's nature's way of giving you an opportunity to deal with unresolved issues. If you have no unresolved issues it's highly likely you'll sail through this time with ease. If on the other hand you've avoided dealing with some emotions they may confront you at this time under the guise of rage, mood swings and/or depression. Whilst I am totally in favour of assisting women through this time the use of some drugs such as hormone replacement therapy only encourage further suppression of these emotions. If you need to use hormone replacement, or something similar, just be aware to deal with your emotions as well. Studies have shown that repressed emotions over time can lead to higher incidences of cancer, heart disease and other illnesses. Caroline Myss says, 'Biography becomes biology'.

I know from personal experience the havoc that hormonal imbalance can cause, and I am not denying it exists. Even so, *you cannot feel an emotion that wasn't inside you in the first place*. As Wayne Dyer says, 'You can't squeeze an orange and get lemon juice'. Hormonal imbalances simply allow what's within to come to the surface. Only by allowing yourself to feel these emotions can you become free of them.

Anger is an emotion that is commonly repressed because it's socially unacceptable. Often behind anger is another emotion. Menopause provided me with the opportunity to get in touch with my real feelings about being a single parent. Up until that time I didn't realise how sad I felt because of all that I had missed. I never had any of the celebrations that most people take for granted; like an engagement or wedding. The births of my children were never celebrated by anyone other than myself; I never experienced sharing any of those happy moments our children bring with someone who loved them as much as I did. And after the initial support provided by family and friends when my son died I was left alone with my grief.

I felt angry, hurt and sad about a lot of things that I'd never acknowledged until menopause brought feelings of absolute rage to the surface. I was shocked at how a nice, positive person like me could feel that way and I went from being a normal, well-balanced positive woman to an angry, negative and frustrated woman. At first I didn't recognise what the real issues were until I worked with the Ten Steps, and was honest with myself about how I really felt and acted on my *being* values, then the symptoms of menopause began to disappear.

Baby boomers, the largest group in history, will enter menopause around the same time and the emotions that these women will experience during that time will have a huge impact on society as a whole. If more women become aware and use this time as an opportunity to heal their past, it will have a very positive impact on society. If they continue to suppress their real feelings the consequences of those choices will affect us all in some way as we are all influenced by group energy.

It may be tempting to skip this step—it's not an easy one to deal with. However, if you find you are continually going around in circles, experiencing the same old problems, you need to access any emotions that keep you bonded to your pain and release them. You cannot change what you don't acknowledge.

There are ways that we can encourage ourselves to acknowledge our underlying emotions—to face our fears—that I have outlined below. I do urge you again however that if you feel you have a major emotional issue then consult a professional counsellor or therapist to help you through the process.

You can allow your feelings to surface by:

Modifying your habits. Don't do what you would normally do. If your way of avoiding pain is to eat, drink, talk, sleep or work then don't do it and allow the fear or pain to surface instead.

Listening to your body. Ask your body what it's trying to tell you when you want to eat, drink and so on. The desire for food, even when you aren't really hungry, can be a way of masking your anger or fear.

Acknowledging fear, anger and guilt. Anger comes from fear and causes guilt. This tight-knit trio commonly holds us back. Women, in particular, are uncomfortable showing anger because they are conditioned to be nurturers and anger goes against everything they are supposed to stand for. So they, and many men too, feel bad about feeling angry so then guilt is added to their list of 'bad' emotions. I believe anger is behind road rage, crime, abuse and even hormonal imbalance.

John Gray summarises it this way, 'Anger results from what happened to you. Sadness is what didn't happen, and sorrow is what could never happen'.

Release the pain from your life

In order to release emotions you need to take some form of action. For some people writing in a journal helps. One way to do this is to write down what you are angry about. If you don't know, write down what you could possibly be angry about. During this process continue to write whatever comes to mind—don't edit your thoughts or words, and don't show them to anyone else. Allow the feelings to pour out of you. When you're finished don't read back over what you have written and, whatever you do, don't write a letter to anyone telling them how you feel. The purpose of this exercise is to face the past and let it go—not to blame someone. You may only need to do this exercise once, or you may need to do it for weeks. Over time as you write about your feelings the intensity of your emotions will subside, and you will sense when it's time to move on. I suggested to one of my clients that her financial problems may stem from the fact that she had not dealt with the death of a close family member, and I recommended she try this exercise. She said that for the first two days whenever she sat down to write she found that no memories out of the ordinary came to her. She thought the whole exercise was pointless. However, she was committed to change and persisted and by the third day she started remembering events and feelings that she had long forgotten.

Talk your problems out of you—when you are alone. This helps if writing doesn't appeal to you. Go for a drive in your car alone, somewhere without much traffic, and where you can pull over if you need to, and say everything you have ever wanted to say—cry, rave, scream—just let the hurt out.

Change the way you think about the problem. If you experience any type of recurring pattern, such as being betrayed by people you love, or being made the scapegoat at work, it's easy to fall into feeling and acting like a victim. Rather than blame the other party for what they've done to you, think about the wonderful opportunity they've given you.

For more than thirty years I attracted people to me who confirmed my belief that people I love abandon me in my time of greatest need, or they betray me. When I realised that these people were in my life to remind me that I needed to change an erroneous belief, I felt differently about them. I believe that on a soul level these people love me, and that's why they kept presenting me with opportunities to change a belief that was holding me back from being all that I could be. Once I changed the way I thought about them and myself I felt liberated. I don't blame myself for being so slow to understand: I am proud of myself because I was so committed to changing this pattern that I kept on repeating it until I finally understood. It took me a long time but I finally got it.

Allow a time for grieving. You can't let go of the past until you've grieved for it so allow yourself to feel the sadness and sorrow. Before you do this you may find it helpful to write a list of some positive ways of consoling yourself while going through this process. This list should include things that make you feel good such as; exercise, music, massage, hugs and so on. This support that you provide for yourself will protect you from feeling overwhelmed by your emotions and can prevent you from slipping back into habits that help you to avoid the pain.

Forgiveness is the pathway to freedom

Once you have faced the fear and grieved for the past, let it go. Stop talking about it, stop reliving it—release the hold your past has on you. Forgive everyone you need to and then move on, although this is often easier to say than do.

My interpretation of forgiveness changed dramatically after reading the book, Radical Forgiveness[6], by Colin C. Tipping. We can be willing to forgive, or intend to forgive but when nothing really changes in your life you may not be forgiving fully. Colin Tipping describes these instances as 'Mock Forgiveness' and 'Pseudo Forgiveness'. In his book he says:

> *'Mock Forgiveness is palliative in nature and built on the shifting sands of illusion.... Mock Forgiveness offers itself as a way of living in the world while Radical Forgiveness is nothing less than a spiritual path....*
>
> *'Pseudo Forgiveness is just neatly packaged judgement and concealed resentment masquerading as forgiveness. However, the line between this and Mock Forgiveness may not be easy to determine and will depend on the consciousness of the person forgiving.'*

Colin gives examples of false forgiveness when you:

Forgive out of a sense of obligation

Forgive out of a sense of righteousness

Bestow forgiveness or pardon

Pretend forgiveness

Make excuses

Real forgiveness begins in your heart. When forgiveness is authentic you can love the people that hurt you, even if you don't like them or don't want to associate with them again. Real forgiveness transforms your life dramatically and it can happen in an instant.

Once you have forgiven you are able to let go, move on and leave the hurt behind. If you're not prepared to forgive, you're not prepared to let go of the pain.

Forgiveness has nothing to do with the other person—it's about you. When you forgive someone, you release their power over you. Forgiveness, therefore, is the most liberating thing you can do for yourself. If you have trouble forgiving the act, which is often the case in instances of sexual abuse, or violent crime, try what Garry Lynch did and forgive the souls of the offenders.

I met Garry and Peg Lynch when I interviewed them for a story that I was writing. Their daughter Anita was raped and murdered by five men while on her way home from work—the crime was so savage there was a public outcry, calling for the death penalty. It would be normal for Anita's parents to feel as if their lives had been ruined by this tragedy, instead they created an opportunity to help others. Garry and Peg now contact parents of murder victims to help them through the difficult early days. At one stage Garry was on the Serious Offender's Review Board being the only civilian, along with judges and specialists in crime and punishment, who decide whether serious offenders should be given early release. Garry has met with prisoners and has actively worked towards rehabilitation for these people, not simply punishment. Both Peg and Garry meditate regularly for world peace.

Garry allowed himself to experience the whole gamut of emotions that result from such a tragedy. This, combined with his willingness to forgive, enabled him to move on.

As I was leaving the Lynch's home Garry shared this story with me.

Garry's Story

Outside our bedroom window is a rose bush which gives off the most beautiful perfume. Although the roses still bloom every year, the perfume disappeared the day after Anita died.

One day I grabbed the rose bush and gave it a shake saying, 'Hey, it's alright. No grief, no unhappiness, only joy now. Okay, joy! Got it?'.

The next day the perfume returned and has remained ever since.

Joy always follows sadness—if you let it.

Sometimes when you've walked through the fire the last thing you feel like doing is looking for an opportunity, but opportunity is the gift you give yourself.

Your opportunity is to change any limiting belief

Once you've completed the process of facing your fears you need to change any limiting beliefs so that you can prevent the same situations from recurring, and you do this by living according to your *being* values.

When you feel tempted to wallow in negative emotions, then act on your chosen values by asking yourself how a powerful (or whatever value you choose) person would act in this situation—then act accordingly. Remember, by acting on your *being* values regularly you are able to change your limiting beliefs. The following are some suggestions for you to think about.

Emotions that keep you bonded to your pain	**Emotions that allow you to heal**	**Values that allow you to change limiting beliefs**
Blame	*Anger*	*Responsible*
Hate		*Loving*
Resentment		*Kind*
Anxiety	*Fear*	*Courageous*
Self pity		*Responsible*
Guilt	*Sadness*	*Accepting*
Doubt		*Determined*
Depression	*Sorrow*	*Cheerful*
Hopelessness		*Resourceful*
Helplessness		*Strong*
Indifference		*Considerate*
Unworthiness		*Wise*

By facing your fears you free yourself from your past and begin to believe that it's possible for you to have everything that you've always wanted.

Walk a new path

At a seminar participants were asked to write very briefly on a card the story of their lives. This is what Portia Nelson wrote[7]:

I walk down a footpath, there's a hole in the path. I don't see it, I fall in. It's not my fault.

I walk down a footpath, there's a hole in the path. I see it, I fall in again. It is my fault.

I walk down a footpath, there's a hole in the path. I fall in again. I get out again immediately.
I walk down a footpath, there is a hole in the path. I walk around it.
I walk down a new street.

This is your time to choose a new street.

Step Six

Create from within first

If you don't go within you'll go without.
—Neale Donald Walsch

So many people think that if they simply work harder or longer they will be able to create more abundance, and perhaps some of us have done just that but it doesn't work for everyone, and it doesn't work all of the time. Some people work incredibly hard yet they struggle to survive let alone achieve their grander dreams. This occurs because we create our reality on the inside first, then we manifest our desires in the physical realm.

This is an important point to understand because sometimes we can mistakenly believe that our power comes from status, money and/or material possessions. When you have this belief your world can suddenly be turned upside down by the loss of a job, a marriage breakdown, or bankruptcy, usually resulting in a feeling of powerlessness.

Real power comes from within and has nothing to do with how much money, opportunity, or intelligence you have. Every thing, the chair you're sitting in, the car you drive, this book you are reading was at one time just an idea. The way to turn our ideas into reality is by going within regularly and connecting with our spirit on a regular basis.

If I told you that in order for you to have everything that you wanted, all you need to do is allocate twenty minutes a day, wouldn't you jump at the opportunity? We all would. And you can do this by taking the time to go within each day. Finding a quiet time to meditate, relax, or simply walk alone is an important step and the one most people don't bother to follow. I can only assume that's because they don't really believe it's possible to have everything they want.

Those who don't take the time to do this often have a whole lot of reasons as to why they couldn't find the time. If this is the case for you think about how much time you spend creating the life that you don't want by searching for solutions, talking about problems or feeling sorry for yourself.

Take a moment to imagine what your life would be like if you knew you could have everything you want. In fact, I highly recommend you put this book down as soon as you finish this paragraph and spend just two minutes daydreaming about that great life. Think about how you would feel, imagine the joy of getting up each day eager to spend another day doing what you love, with the people you love.

Take this one step further and imagine that everyone else is able to have all that they desire as well. What a different place the world would be. There would be no need for crime because everyone would have all the love, money, power and attention that they crave. There would be no need for violence, power struggles or office politics, and there would be no need for war.

I've asked clients to do this exercise and noticed their features soften and their bodies relax as they imagine having everything they have always wanted. Often they comment on how much lighter they feel. Without exception they all look happier. When you give yourself permission to have everything you want, you feel real happiness—and isn't that the way life is supposed to be?

Doing without doesn't help you create what you want because when you feel deprived most of your energy is focused on what you don't have, what you're doing wrong, or how to change your situation—and whatever you focus on you attract. When your focus is on problems, doubts and fears you continually manifest more of the same. The world has been struggling with this issue for centuries and it's time to end the struggle.

Life doesn't have to be hard. The abundance of this wonderful universe we inhabit is not just for the chosen, or the good—it's for everyone. You can have what you want. The key is that no-one else can give it to you—you create it for yourself by going within regularly and being congruent with your thoughts, words and actions.

How to go within

Going within each day enables you to connect with your spirit. I believe my spirit is the part of me that never dies. Not all of my clients share my beliefs and that's okay. However, I still encourage them to take the time to go within each day and everyone who does this comments on the changes that show up in their lives, and how much easier their life flows.

Meditation will take you to a level of experience that will make many of your concerns seem trivial. When I first asked for what I wanted in my meditation, fully believing I could have it, I experienced a state of ecstasy that is beyond anything I've ever felt before or since. I meditate daily, mostly because it makes me feel good and it helps my day run more smoothly, it also helps me to create a life that I love. It's a positive way of shutting out the busyness of the world and allowing myself time to be aware of what's really important to me.

You don't need any special skills to meditate. It's not necessary to attend classes. All that is required is for you to make time to sit quietly. Close your eyes and let whatever thoughts and feelings enter your mind then let them drift away without force. This may take some practise but it does get easier over time. If you have something particular that you want to manifest in your life either ask for it at the outset, or visualise yourself as already having what you desire. It's only by taking a quiet time regularly that you have the opportunity to listen to your inner voice.

At one time I was confused about what work I wanted to do and felt as if I was going around in circles, not getting any closer to a solution, so I asked for guidance in my daily meditation. I even went so far as to say, *Just send someone into my life to tell me what to do and I will do it.* Two days later I received a letter from a book reader, in which she advised me she was psychic and that she had a feeling during a meditation to contact me as I was confused as to what direction to go in—she offered to give me a free reading.

Well, I was so excited and amazed at this response that I called her straight away.

I had to wait two weeks to see her. The day finally arrived and I was eager to be told what to do. She suggested that I bring along photographs of people in my life, so I could ask any questions about them, which I did. I spent two hours with her. Although she was a lovely person, I was thoroughly disappointed because nothing in the reading, or any comments that she made about the people in the photographs, related to my life at all. The whole reading sounded as if she was talking about someone else. And, in the time since that reading, which was a few years ago now, none of the predictions have even remotely come true.

Later that night I asked during my quiet time what the meeting was all about. The answer I received was that no-one could tell me my future *because it's not pre-ordained.* My future is what I choose it to be. This whole incident may seem to be a contradiction of what I've said about asking for guidance, however, I do believe that my meeting with this woman was no accident, her purpose in my life was to remind me that I can't give responsibility for my life away to someone else.

Some people may wonder how you can ask a question and receive an answer. After asking a question some people have a feeling as to what they should do. Others like myself, hear an inner voice. We all have thoughts and carry on an internal dialogue however, I've found that my inner voice is different. I can usually differentiate between a thought and an intuition. This is not psychic phenomena, it's a skill that I've developed over time. Every time I fail to listen to my inner voice I regret it. Sometimes you may dream about the situation and the solution is obvious. There are times when answers come instantly and other times when weeks or even months pass before clarity dawns. A lot of the time I've noticed that someone comes into my life with just the solution, help, guidance or idea that is exactly what I need.

A number of people over the years have told me what their psychics have predicted. Unfortunately sometimes these people have put their lives on hold waiting for some future event to happen. The whole experience with the psychic was very liberating for me as from that moment on I stopped looking for answers outside of myself. As I focused on creating my own answers the clearer the Ten Steps upon which this book is based became, and as a result of practising those steps I became aware of what I wanted to do with my life.

It has been scientifically proven that meditation can reduce blood pressure, release stress and promote a feeling of well being. The form of meditation that I practise most often is one Wayne Dyer teaches on the CD, *Meditations for Manifesting*[8]. This particular meditation allows the meditator to reach a level of Siddhi consciousness using sound.

According to Wayne Dyer, '*Siddhi* consciousness is a perfect state of awareness in which there is a complete absence of doubt and no delay between the origination of a thought and its materialisation into the world of form'.[9]

Sounds are a powerful source of energy, the vibration from particular sounds can lift you to higher levels of consciousness, and in the case of Siddhi consciousness, the vibrations produced take you to the level of manifestation. This may seem far fetched to some people and all I can say is try it first to see if it works for you as it has for me and many others. Some people also find that by focusing on a sound it makes it easier to tune out distracting everyday thoughts.

Siddhi meditation

The ideal time to do this meditation is first thing in the morning, so that you program your day the way you want it to be. Sit somewhere quiet and comfortable, close your eyes and relax.

Begin with a mental picture of what you want—your choice can be small or large, it doesn't matter—there's no need to limit yourself, so be guided by your *having* values. Place your attention on the feeling, that is how you want to feel once you manifest this desire.

As you take a deep breath in imagine the energy flowing through your body from your root chakra, which is where your sexual organs are located, proceeding up through your body, clearing your energy field until it reaches your third eye, which is located between your eyebrows.

Exhale slowly and as you release your breath make the sound '*aahh*'. As you do this, imagine your energy flowing from your third eye, circling what you desire. Keep your focus on how you would feel having your desire, rather than on visualising the manifestation of a specific thing.

As you breathe in deeply again, draw that feeling of well-being, triumph, happiness or whatever the emotion is into your body and repeat the process.

It's easy to get caught up in doing this meditation precisely, however it helps to know that there is no right way or wrong way. You can make the '*aahh*' sound out loud at high volume or you can say it softly, or you can say it to yourself.

Like any new skill it may take practise to master. You may not feel like anything is happening at first, however, changes may be occurring subtly at first, just persist with daily practise and watch what happens.

When I first started working with this meditation I wanted to sell a small business I owned. I wanted to sell the business with just one advertisement, for the right price and to someone who really needed it. I took this request into my '*aahh*' meditation for approximately three days before placing the advertisement, visualising the right buyer coming into my life and feeling how good it would feel to be able to move onto work that I really loved.

As a result of that advertisement Frances was the first person to ring me and she came to see me the next day. I received other phone calls although none of them sounded interested enough to be prospective buyers. Frances said she was interested but wanted to think about it. Towards the end of that week I thought about placing another advertisement, but decided against it. I knew that if I really believed I could sell the business with one advertisement that I needed to ensure my actions supported that belief. Over the next two weeks Frances came back to see me twice, although she still didn't make a commitment. I must admit I was really tempted to run the advertisement again, but I resisted and waited and continued with my daily meditation. And it worked. Four weeks after I placed that one advertisement Frances signed the contract. She was the only person that I showed the business to and it was perfect for her.

When you can't or don't want to meditate

Some people simply can't or don't want to meditate, so I suggest that you find another way to go within.

Jim Vuocolo, a life coach and minister says that he can't meditate because he has attention deficit disorder (ADD). So, instead of conventional meditation, he uses driving to switch off his conscious mind. He gets into his car by himself and as he drives, his brainwaves slow down to an alpha state—the same as is achieved during meditation. This may sound dangerous but it's normal that when we do any activity that we are really familiar with that doesn't require conscious thought, such as taking a shower or driving, to automatically go into an alpha state.

Jim also found that, because of his ADD, he couldn't focus enough to pray and sitting still in church drove him crazy. So, he became a minister—this way he prays by preaching sermons out loud to his congregation, and achieves the same end benefit for himself.

If you prefer to be active while you go within, yoga, tai chi or walking alone for example can be a form of meditation and bring the same benefits into your life.

Visualisation

Visualisation is another process that allows you to quiet the mind, while you mentally see your life the way you want it to be. Some of my clients visualise and meditate, like David whose story I told earlier, and others feel more comfortable just visualising.

The best way to do this is to find a quiet place and simply relax, close your eyes and breathe deeply. Once you feel relaxed you can create in your imagination a sanctuary (real or imaginary), a place where you can go to dream.

Put yourself into this special place, and while there, imagine your life the way you want it to be. See yourself as already having, or doing, all that you've chosen for yourself. Visualise the way you want look and include the people you want to share your life with. Add in as much detail as possible even down to colours and sounds.

Some people prefer to listen to a tape that guides their visualisation; this helps the mind to stop wandering. One tape I've found particularly helpful is by Craig Townsend. This guided visualisation is only twelve minutes long, which makes it ideal for beginners, and it tells you step-by-step what to do.

Visualisation is an effective and simple tool that can be used to create the life you want any time and anywhere.

It doesn't matter how you manage to go within, so experiment until you find a way that suits you and make it a part of your daily life.

Step Seven

Success lies in your daily habits

You should design the things you don't like right out of your future.

— Barbara Sher

I once listened to a tape by Raymond Aaron, a Canadian motivational speaker, in which he said, 'Make your inside match your outside'. I love that expression because it so clearly highlights what many people don't do to help themselves. Think about this, how often have you set goals and then allowed your daily words and actions contradict what you want? For instance, you may want to have lots of money, you may dress the part and look like you're worth a million dollars however, you worry constantly about money, how you're going to pay the bills and keep up appearances. If you recognise this or similar situations then your inside doesn't match your outside.

You create from within first with your thoughts and words, and then you create in the physical realm with your actions. To create the life you really want you need to think and speak as if you already have all that you've chosen as covered in Step Four.You now need to act as if you already have all that you've chosen and you can do this by reassessing every area of your life.

Becoming congruent

The process of establishing congruence can be likened to a mental and physical spring-clean, and just like when you paint a room and then notice how shabby the carpet looks, the more you progress with your personal spring-cleaning you may notice that you'll find there is more to be done.

Don't be overwhelmed by the prospect of this perpetual spring-cleaning—there is always a way to find the time, and to reduce stress in the process. Ultimately your reward will be so much more time and energy.

To help you design your future, you need to develop habits that enable you to think, talk and act in a way that confirms that you will have all of your desires.

Lydia's story

I work from home as a freelance writer. Working from home has some great benefits, I can work my own hours, dress the way I want and I don't have to worry about office politics. However, there was once a downside for me as well.The spare bedroom was my office, it was also was the dumping ground for the washing wait-

ing to be ironed, kid's toys and any other paraphernalia that didn't have another home.

At one stage I wanted more work, I love writing, but a part of me was also wishing it away because I didn't feel like I could cope with any more. In addition to this feeling of not being able to cope, I often worked myself into a panic whenever clients wanted to drop in and talk to me about a project, because my office was a mess. I felt I always had to travel to see them, which took up more of my time.

Time and money were my enemies. I needed more money so that I could employ a cleaner and have more help around the house, but I didn't have the time to take on any more work. I didn't think I had the time to spend on becoming congruent, it was desperation that finally drove me to make the effort and I transformed my life in the process.

I set aside half an hour at the beginning of each day to restore order in my office. I must admit I began this task without a great deal of confidence at first. As the room started improving, I decided to have shelving installed and a new power point put in, this made my work area much more manageable.

The next thing I tackled was the wardrobe. I was ruthless—throwing out old roller skates, games, tennis rackets that would never be used again. Once the wardrobe was emptied, I created an orderly storage system and I had a lot more space than I realised.

The office was looking so good I decided to repaint it and to get rid of anything that made it look like a bed-

room. I sold the spare bed and replaced it with a sofa bed. I changed, the pictures on the wall and my office ended up looking very professional, a space where I would be proud to see clients.

It took three weeks, working at it half an hour a day, every day. The transformation was incredible and well worth the effort.

Shortly afterwards I landed a new contract writing a regular newsletter. I love the work and the extra money meant I could pay for more help around the home.I realised that I'd been sending out mixed messages previously. I needed more work and at the same time I didn't want it because I felt overloaded, and I didn't want people coming to my home. Now I am aware of how important it is to be congruent all the time. It didn't really take that much effort to put my office in order and my office and my income now reflect the professional that I am.

How you treat yourself, your working environment, your home and possessions says a lot about you to others. Whether we like it or not, people make judgements based on appearances.

Another client made a comment on how she felt she looked shabby, and perhaps on occasions she was right. This woman wanted to expand her business in the area of personal development, but no matter how hard she tried her business failed to grow. I can only assume, considering the principles of congruence, that part of her problem was that new clients may have thought she couldn't be very good at her job if she made so little money that she couldn't afford decent clothes.

When I first took over a franchise for my financial planning business I had very little money and leased the cheapest office I could find. While I saw a lot of clients, only a small percentage of those clients placed their investments through me. As my income came mostly from commissions, that meant I didn't make a lot of money. Slowly however, with persistence my business grew and as I made more money I kept upgrading my office. It wasn't until I moved into a really nice office that my business started to prosper. I now understand that I held myself back by saying that people had to accept me as I am. Would you give your money to an investment adviser that looked poor? I probably wouldn't.

Admittedly at first I didn't have the money to spend on a nice office but there were other options that I could have chosen, such as sharing an office, that would have enabled me to reach my goals sooner.

Being congruent is an important step, and I am not suggesting that you live beyond your means, or buy clothes and cars that you can't afford in order to impress others—because that would mean allowing the tribe to influence your choices. Begin by focusing on making your thoughts and words match, then tackle one area of your life at a time and establish congruence as much as you are able, and if there are limitations look at alternative ways to achieve the same end result.

You might begin by working to establish congruence in your relationships in order to create more harmony.

Congruence can help you create harmonious relationships

If you want harmonious relationships act as if you already have them now. One way you can do this is by not criticising, or talking judgementally about others. Remind yourself, whenever you feel tempted to do this, that the temporary relief you gain from indulging in the habit of talking about others or gossiping, is not worth the long term consequences.

When you take a moment to consider what criticism really is, you'll realise that it's just ego wanting to be better than someone else. Most people have to bring other people down in order to build themselves up. Rather than trying to change another we can give them the gift of acceptance, which is more precious than anything material.

In order to change a habit you need to first be aware of it, and secondly develop strategies to put in place whenever you find yourself returning to that old habit. The next time you find yourself engaged in gossip or criticising another, change the subject by saying something like, 'That's their right' and move onto another subject.

If you believe in the principle of oneness, that is that we are all connected at some level, then you cannot damage another without hurting yourself. Cancer is the result of a diseased cell attacking the other cells, until it destroys the whole, including itself. When you refuse to live in harmony with those in your life, when you insist that your view is right, then you are effectively acting in the same way as a cancer cell. Ultimately you will destroy your own happiness as well as the relationships in your life.

The following suggestions will help to create harmonious relationships.

Forgive everyone. One of my clients who is very successful in showbusiness made a daily habit of forgiving everyone in her life. There was nothing that she considered too trivial to be included in her daily acts of forgiveness. If someone irritated her and she found herself having critical thoughts towards them, she would forgive them in her daily meditation.

Make amends. When I was redesigning my life I decided to make amends to people I may have offended. I sat down one day and wrote letters of apology to three people. I had no intention of re-establishing a relationship with them, I just wanted to clear up the past. I didn't hear from any of the people and I didn't want to. However, there was an enormous difference in how I felt about myself. I felt as if I was living according to my *being* values.

Make a list of things that have been done to you that you dislike, and don't do these things to other people. Being ignored used to be a big issue for me, and certain people in my life used it as a form of manipulation. There was a time in my life when I was very manipulative, although I wasn't always aware of it. Nowadays I make a point of not manipulating. I also decided that being treated in this way did not match who I am, and I refused to accept this behaviour any longer. As a consequence most of those people have now left my life. This doesn't bother me because they've been replaced by people I have a great deal of respect for.

Make a list of things that have been done for you that you like, and do these for other people. When I ran a magazine, I had a number of opportunities to communicate with Dottie Walters, who went out of her way to be helpful. Dottie runs the largest speaking bureau in the US and publishes the magazine *Sharing Ideas*, as well as being a successful speaker and author of several books. What I admire most about Dottie is that she always has time to make a suggestion even though she is a very busy, successful woman—so I decided to do the same for others, and I can't tell you how much that's changed my relationships. Where once people used to criticise me I now receive positive support, encouragement and words of kindness every week.

Practise being kind rather than right. Think about how often you may put down the people you love in order to prove yourself right. How often do you have to have the last word? How often do you have to win the argument, forgetting in the process the damage that choice has on your relationship?

Praise others. I'm not suggesting you say anything that you don't mean. Just remember that when someone does something you like, to tell them how much you appreciate it.

My eldest daughter had a new person start at her work. This man took over a lot of her duties and did far more than was expected, he worked through his lunch hour and generally made Lisa's life a whole lot easier. Every night she would come home singing his praises. One night I asked her if she had told him how much she appreciated his help and she said she hadn't thought of it. The next day she told him how much she appreciated him and his response was to tell her how she'd made his day. Appreciation costs nothing and you will be the one to benefit the most from it. This is because what you give out comes back to you.

Sometimes we forget about telling those closest to us just how much we admire them. When I was selecting the character traits of the person that I want to be I chose kind, loving and generous after observing my daughter Lisa. Lisa demonstrates all of those qualities daily, she truly is a beautiful person, as is my youngest daughter Laura. As parents we get so used to telling our kids what to do, and reminding them about what they haven't done, that it's easy to forget to tell them just how great they really are. I certainly made Lisa's week when I told her that I had chosen to be just like her.

Once you begin to establish harmony you might next decide to put your finances in order. Money is always a good area to establish congruence in early on, as money, or the lack of it, affects nearly every area of your life.

Create more money in your life

Some people spend their life in crisis management. When one problem is solved and they have time to work on creating the life they really want, another financial disaster occurs. This is a way of avoiding dealing with the real issues.

Your first priority is to establish an income. You cannot create from nothing and if you simply don't have enough to live on your priority is to find a way to generate an income while you are working towards what you really desire (refer 'Create a launching pad' in Step Two). You don't need to love every job you do, we can put up with anything when we know that it's a short term solution that's taking us where we want to be. When your focus is constantly on survival it's hard to create abundance.

Live within your means. Everyone of us needs to know how much money comes in and how much goes out. It sounds obvious but many people don't know and you can't make any choices until you have this information at your fingertips. You can't pass the buck on this one, even to your spouse, because ultimately the only person who is responsible for you is you. Over the years I've met many women whose husbands have handled the finances; that's okay if it works for you, but you still need to know where your money goes. This will protect you if your circumstances should ever change.

Earlier I suggested that it's not necessary to deprive yourself, and I want to emphasise that I'm not encouraging you to spend money that you don't have. This is because eventually the focus shifts from pleasure, to worrying about how you're going pay the bills. What I am suggesting is that you pamper yourself within your means. There are many ways to indulge yourself that don't cost money. For instance, you can enjoy a luxuriating bubble bath, borrow a good book from the library or go for a walk in a beautiful area—all of these can give you a feeling of wellbeing and they cost little or nothing.

Clear your debts. The best thing to do with debts is get rid of them, and there are a number of ways you can do this.

1. If you're behind in loan repayments and you have not already done so, you need to contact your creditors and make arrangements for a payment schedule that you can manage.

2. If you have a good credit record and the capacity to repay a loan, it may be better to consolidate all of your debts into one loan. This usually reduces your monthly commitment and will give you more disposable income.
3. Allocate twenty per cent of your income (if this is possible) towards clearing debt. Make the minimum repayment on all loans, then allocate any remaining money to the debt with the highest interest rate and so on. When this loan has been repaid, use the money to pay off the next debt with the highest interest rate. If you keep making the same repayments even when you have less debts—you'll eliminate your debts in record time and gain a feeling of personal satisfaction in the process.

One client managed to repay twenty five thousand dollars in debts in just one year by taking on a second job and living on a very strict budget. You wouldn't want to do this for too long but one year was sufficient for Sally to be able to eliminate the burden of debt so that she could focus on buying a home of her own.

Make a plan. It's wise to keep three months' living expenses in investments or the bank, or have three months living expenses available to you via a redraw facility on your mortgage, that way you never have to worry about money if something unexpected should happen. If you don't have this much money readily available make a plan similar to the one used to reduce debt.

I always suggest that you never plan for emergencies. Remember, what you focus on you attract I do recommend however, that you put some money aside for opportunities, or you may prefer to think of this as your peace of mind money.

Create Order. I cannot emphasise enough how important order is to change how you feel about money. Order means that you set up some type of system for filing, accounts (paid and to be paid) and taxation records.

Some of the things that you can do are:

- Throw out old receipts/papers, usually anything over five years old. The Australian Taxation Office requires personal records to be kept for five years and business records to be kept for seven years. Retain papers pertinent to current loans or investments and file in a safe place.
- Do your tax returns.
- Reassess your bank accounts. The more bank accounts you have the more charges you pay, so as a general rule two to three bank accounts is ample. One for general living expenses, one for savings and possibly one for bills. If you are disciplined enough to manage with one it's best to do so.
- Seek financial advice if you have more than three months' living expenses in the bank. Too many people keep large amounts of money in bank savings accounts that only earn one or two percent interest. This money can be invested in many different ways that can give you a better return on your savings. By valuing every dollar it helps your money to grow into larger amounts. A good financial planner can help you create a prosperous future.

- Make a will. Let the executor of your will, or appropriate family member, know where your records are kept.

It will take time to fully implement this plan; don't let that stop you from working on other areas of your life at the same time. Think about how you would act if you knew you could have everything you want and it's only just a matter of time. Once you've done this *act* as if all of your dreams are about to come true within the next twelve months by preparing now.

Remember, your priority is to establish order: this reduces stress and allows you to attract opportunities to you.

Enjoy your work

Create order. We spend around a quarter of our lives at work so it makes sense to enjoy whatever you do. You can go about creating order and becoming more organised in much the same way as you handle your personal finances, this will help to reduce stress, allowing you to have more energy to be creative in your job and thus have more enjoyment.

Communicate your needs. Working with others calls for the development of interpersonal skills. Many people fail to see the importance of this or that it's their responsibility. You need to communicate your needs to your bosses and co-workers.

If you hate your job, set a date by which you intend to leave. This does not mean that you have to give notice, in fact I highly recommend that you tell no-one about this date. This is a psychological deadline that helps you to make plans to improve your situation. You can move this deadline forward or backwards at any time you choose. If you don't make any plans to create what you really want you may find yourself, years later, still stuck in a job that you hate.

Remember, that passion and work go hand in hand—over the long term, don't settle for less than you really want.

Treat others the way you know they can be. Barbara attended one of my seminars and shared this story with the group.

Barbara's story

I work for a large insurance company where it's the office junior's job to put away stationery. For a period of time a number of large boxes full of stationery were left in the corridors, inconveniencing everyone.

For days the boxes remained where they were and I felt really annoyed about this and often complained about how lazy the office junior was.

One day after I'd complained again, one of the other girls in the office who is much younger than me commented, 'Maybe she doesn't know how to be organised. Why don't we show her?'.

I've always considered myself to be a kind person, and it was only when my colleague made that comment that I realised how foolishly I'd been acting. I decided that in future I would lead by example. My colleague and I offered to help put the stationery away and to show this girl how she could work more efficiently. When we did this order was restored in a harmonious way.

Goethe says, 'If you treat an individual as if he were what he ought to be and could be, he will become what he ought to be and could be'.

Adopt healthy habits

The good things in life lose their meaning if you are not healthy, so establishing healthy habits is vital to long term enjoyment of life.

Find a way to enjoy exercise. For most of my life I hated exercise. I now walk regularly and have done so for the past couple of years. It took me some time to discover a form of exercise that was enjoyable for me instead of feeling like I should be doing this or some other exercise regime. I actually enjoy these quiet times by myself and often get my best ideas during these periods. If walking doesn't appeal to you take up some activity that you enjoy like dancing or a sport.

Small changes add up to big changes. Change one thing at a time then keep building on those changes. That way you are likely to be motivated by these small achievements to choose goals that may be further out of reach, rather than feeling overwhelmed by the list of things you want to change.

Focus on the process, not the outcome. At one time I worked with a personal trainer and I remember him saying, 'Don't focus on how much weight you have lost, because once you've achieved your goal you'll drop all of the good habits you have acquired. Focus on the process instead and the rest will follow.'

Re-evaluate your appearance. How do you feel about the way you look? If you're not happy with your appearance do something about it. Remember, that if you don't like something you can change it, and that includes your dress, hair, weight and general appearance.

Perhaps it's not so much a physical change that needs to take place it may be that you need to change the way you feel about how you look. Very few people look like models, we come in all shapes and sizes and that's what makes us unique.

Create your lifestyle

The key to living a great life is to add some of the things you've always wanted into your life today. Don't wait until your life is perfect, or until you can afford it, you need to have some fun along the way. Just be sure to add these things into your life in a responsible and affordable way so that they remain pleasurable.

Time for fun is important. No matter how much you love your job or your family, there needs to be balance in order to have an happy abundant life. That means that leisure time and fun are essential.

What do you talk about doing one day? Is there a hobby you'd like to take up? What's stopping you from doing it now?

When life gets tough the first things we stop doing are usually all the things that we enjoy. Life doesn't have to be perfect before you can enjoy it.

Make a list of one hundred things that you have always wanted to do and work your way through your list. This list can also include things that you want to have, or be. The more items you have on your list the more likely you are to lead a more fulfilling life. I've found that the clients who have trouble even coming up with even a dozen things are the ones who usually struggle through life.

Clear away the clutter. Cleaning out and giving away what you don't want creates a space for more of what you do want to come into your life. Twice a year I usually clean out most of my cupboards. This includes the kitchen, wardrobes, linen cupboard and garage. The rule I live by is if I haven't used it for two years or more, chances are I won't again. Sure I make mistakes and sometimes find I need something later however, on all but one occasion it has always been something I can replace. This isolated case is far outweighed by the pleasure of opening organised cupboards or being able to find things easily on a daily basis.

A well-meaning friend encouraged me to clean out my son's bedroom the day after he died, while I was still in a state of shock. Just about everything of his was given away and it was too soon for me to be making such decisions. Clearing out doesn't mean you have to give everything away. I now have a policy that I won't part with anything that I'm emotionally attached to, like the occasional favourite item of my children's clothing that I love, or things they've made me, photographs or cards. Now, if these mementos took up an entire wardrobe I may have to reassess that decision, but at this time they fit comfortably into a large memory box.

Create an environment that makes you feel good. If you feel happy about having the bed unmade then leave it, but be honest with yourself. Most of us feel better when our bed is made and our environment is tidy. If you don't have time to do this task everyday then get up ten minutes earlier and get others in your household to help you. This may seem a small point, however if you realise that seeing your bed unmade for example annoys you, or makes you feel overloaded when you arrive home from work, then you will feel inspired by the positive effect such a small change can make.

You don't need to have a lot of money to create a great atmosphere, what's most important is the feeling you get from it.

Create more time

The biggest obstacle we all face is finding the time to make changes to the way we live. If this is a problem for you then you really need to learn to prioritise to help you through the process of change. You need to ask yourself if the way you are living really works for you.

The following are just a few suggestions which may assist you to achieve the results you want without creating too much stress:

Break it down. Nearly every task can be broken down so that you can find the time to begin the process of creating a life you love. When doing major tasks like putting your finances in order, work at it for ten minutes a day if you can't spare an hour or two. Ten minutes a day adds up to over an hour a week. You can use the same principle to ensure there is time in your week for doing things that you love.

I've had clients who say they want to write, so I've suggested they aim for one or two pages a day, rather than ten. One page a day, over a year, would amount to a large book.

If that doesn't appeal, try getting up an hour earlier a day and devote this time solely to your passion.

If you find you continue to procrastinate then you may need to go back and do some work on facing your fears (refer Step Five: Face your fears). And, if the job is too large and beyond your capabilities, hire an organisational consultant or ask a friend to assist you.

As I've mentioned previously most people live their life back to front. They work so they can have money to escape their life. When work is your passion, then you never need to retire and holidays become enjoyable interludes.

Ask others to help you. You can maintain order by implementing five or ten minute clean ups and getting other family members to help you. Set an oven timer and work as quickly as you can putting everything back in its place; put on a load of washing, put out the garbage, wipe down the sink and benches, stack the dishwasher and generally tidy up. Then the whole household can turn it's attention onto more fun things. I heard this suggestion from a guest author on the Oprah Show and found it works really well. If there are four people in your household, and very young children can be included if you make it fun, five minutes per person adds up to twenty minutes a day—and because you're all working at a faster pace than normal that could be the equivalent of forty minutes working alone. This method can be applied to any task such as cleaning out a cupboard, cleaning the car, cleaning up your children's rooms or organising your library. You don't need to do it all alone and it can be fun.

Do more than one thing at a time. Most women are masters at doing two or three things at once, however care needs to be taken in order to avoid stress. When doing multiple tasks ensure that you do things in the one area. For instance, if you are in the kitchen complete work in that room. I can help my daughter Laura with her homework while I am preparing dinner, folding the washing, tidying up the kitchen or cleaning out the fridge.

There are numerous ways you can do more than one thing at a time without trying to be superwoman, and without creating unnecessary stress.

The more efficient you become at managing your time and affairs, the more time you will have for the things that are really important to you. Be creative, for every problem there is a solution.

When you start enjoying life, your energy changes and you'll begin to experience synchronicity on a regular basis. So take the time now to allow more luxuries in and allow more time to do the things you enjoy, or visit the places you have always wanted to go to.

Establish a daily routine

Most of the areas covered in this chapter are related to things that you do on a periodic basis, and they're important. Equally important is what you do on a daily basis.

If you're serious about living a life you love it's important to establish a routine that becomes a part of your daily life. My routine includes daily meditation, saying statements of truth whenever I want something new, giving thanks for what I have now, and for what I know will come, reading inspirational books and listening to inspirational tapes. This routine is as necessary for my spiritual and emotional well-being as food and exercise are for my body.

Keep the following points in mind when setting your daily routine.

- Choose a routine that you can live with, there's no point in creating a routine that you don't enjoy.
- Be wary of taking on too much. If you go overboard and do too much, too soon, you may grow tired of it and give it all away.
- Set aside a specific time. You clean your teeth at around the same time everyday don't you? So, do the same for what's important to you—decide on a time for meditating, saying your statements of truth, or whatever method you use to support your choices.

Eliminate thoughts, words and actions that are not taking you where you want to go. Act on a daily basis as if all of your dreams will come true in the next three months, and watch what happens.

Step Eight

Allow no doubt

Those who are certain of the outcome can afford to wait, and without anxiety.

—Wayne Dyer

As we were driving up our driveway on the way to school one day my daughter, Laura exclaimed, 'Wow, look at the flowers on that tree, aren't they beautiful'. She was referring to our Jacaranda trees which bloomed that day for the first time in seven years. Laura went on to say, 'I always wondered why you planted those trees, they've always looked rather scrawny looking to me'. I explained to Laura that the trees had never had the opportunity to reach their full potential because they were planted in poor soil.

When I first bought our home I had great intentions of creating a beautiful garden. I spent a lot of money on plants only to find that many of them died, and those that did survive didn't reach their full potential. This wasn't because of neglect on my part, I watered and fed my plants regularly but no matter how hard I worked the results were less than spectacular.

Finally I consulted a horticulturist. He told me that no amount or watering or feeding would help my plants to grow as the soil was compacted, in some places it was like concrete. You can understand, this being the case, that the more fragile plants never had a chance, and the stronger trees that persevered found it difficult to survive, let alone thrive.

I wanted a quick fix, an instant garden but it just wasn't possible. We had to dig in bags of clay breaker, lay down copious amounts of compost, fertiliser and mulch, then water regularly and allow nature to transform clay into rich soil. Six months later I replanted my garden, and while it's still young I am now reaping the rewards of laying the right foundation.

Working on yourself is a lot like working on a garden; when you work with your consciousness only—by being positive, setting goals, planning, saying affirmations and using visualisation techniques—the results you get will depend upon what's below the surface.

These are all good things to do, but they won't bring you the results that you desire unless the soil is good. The soil is your unconscious. You need to dig down deep, release the old hurts, heal the wounds, nurture yourself before your new seeds, being your new beliefs, rules and values have a fertile ground in which to take hold.

Most of my clients are people who have done lots of work on themselves. They're very knowledgeable and aware; some of them have spent years reading self-help books, attending seminars and courses or attending counselling. Quite a few have found they can achieve goals, however their success is sometimes short-lived. Once these people achieve a goal it's not uncommon for them to lose ground and actually go backwards for awhile. If you've ever experienced this 'yo-yo cycle' yourself you'll know what I mean. The longer you remain trapped in this cycle the more pain accumulates and the more self-pitying and doubtful you become. After awhile you begin to doubt yourself.

The process of creation involves changing the beliefs and habits of a lifetime. Whenever something goes wrong, understand that there is nothing wrong with you, life is presenting you with another opportunity to change your beliefs, release your pain, forgive or accept your worthiness to receive, in other words to heal. This is your opportunity to make new choices.

Once you become aware and make conscious choices in every area of your life your core beliefs begin to automatically change.

Understanding focus

Focus is what we think, speak and act upon on a daily basis.

When you constantly talk about what you're doing wrong, the problems in your life and your daily irritations, your focus is on what you don't want.

Some people say, 'But I know all that, I *am* positive'. And, in the next breath they tell me how stupid they are, or how hopeless they are or how they've learnt to put up with something. Hardly anyone is as positive as they imagine themselves to be.

Wayne Dyer says, 'Imagine walking into a store and saying, 'What an ugly rug. I hate it. How much is it? I'll take two''. This may sound ridiculous, but it's what we do when we constantly focus on what we don't want.

Let me give you an example of how you do this. Imagine you have a problem getting on with a certain type of person—think about how you normally behave with this person. Do you talk about this person with your family, or friends? Maybe you complain about how this person misunderstands you. You might even make the comment, 'I can't win'. If you behave in this way you just bought the ugly rug.

Imagine you have problems with money, that there is not enough to go around, and to improve this situation you say positive affirmations to attract more money into your life. In between these affirmations you rehearse what you will say to your creditors, or you avoid opening bills because that will only make you depressed, you avoid doing any financial planning because that means you'll have to face up to your current situation.

This type of behaviour is what creates the yo-yo cycle because there is no congruence. When your thoughts, words and actions are in conflict you experience success sometimes and failure at others times. This is why I say things don't just happen to you, a lot of the time you unconsciously create the very situation you complain about.

The yo-yo cycle stems from a lack of trust in yourself and your own power. It's just another opportunity to change a limiting belief.

Think back to when you first learnt to ride a bike; you probably felt really excited until a doubt entered your mind, at that stage you most likely lost your balance. I can remember teaching my youngest daughter Laura to rollerblade. She was skating along just fine, albeit slowly when she said to me, 'I can almost rollerblade'. I said, 'You are rollerblading now'. That's when she fell over, because she didn't really believe she could skate alone—she wasn't ready to trust herself.

Trusting is not a feeling—it is action.

Children are born trusting however it doesn't take us long to knock it out of them. We teach our children about 'stranger danger'; we teach them that God loves them, but only if they keep his laws—if they don't they will go to hell for eternity, and we teach them to protect their possessions or others may take them from them. In other words we teach them fear. I'm not saying that we shouldn't teach our children to protect themselves for not everyone is trustworthy, but we can do it in a way that empowers them.

For those of you who lack trust because of things that have happened in the past, think about this; your past doesn't have to continue to affect your life—your life today is a result of what you put your attention on. Just stay focused on now.

Take care who you share your dreams with

Wayne Dyer suggested at a seminar I attended that it's best not to share your dreams with anyone, not even those people closest to you. When we share our dreams with others, doubts have a fertile breeding ground because well-meaning friends and loved ones often dampen our enthusiasm with a word, a look or even a gesture. When this happens you begin to doubt yourself and as a result your resolve weakens.

As one who loves to talk I found this a radical suggestion and I wondered if I could stop talking about my plans and dreams. I decided I was prepared to try.

On leaving the seminar I ran into some people I know and we all commented on how great the day had been and how much we had learnt. Without thinking I said, 'I really want Wayne Dyer's life'. It was the kind of throwaway remark like many we make in everyday conversation. One of these people turned to me frowning and said, 'You don't really mean that. You don't want to be Wayne Dyer'.

I started explaining that of course I didn't want to be Wayne Dyer. I was quite happy being me. But I went on to tell them that what I really liked about Wayne's life was the three months holiday each year in Hawaii with his family, and so on. Mid-sentence I heard myself justifying what I wanted and quickly changed the subject.

And isn't that what we do everyday? We share our dreams with others, and then feel that we have to justify our desires. We don't have to justify anything to anyone. Only you can decide if you want to keep all of your dreams to yourself, but if you do decide to share them with others, take care choosing who you share them with. When other people express their opinion, they are only telling you about their beliefs, and that doesn't have to be your reality.

It's also tempting for our egos to gain attention by talking about what we plan to do and that can be our pay-off. This does not help you manifest your dreams, it only scatters your energy.

Act on your first thought

In order to change a core belief, you need to act before you think. Yes, this is the opposite to what we've all been taught, and it's not the same as *reacting* as mentioned in Step Two. Acting on your first thought is a conscious choice. Reacting is when you respond automatically without thinking.

The following extract taken from Neale Donald Walsch's book *Conversations with God*[10], explains why you should do this.

> *'You're walking down the street and come across an old lady begging for quarters. You know easily she's a bag lady and is living day-to-day. You instantly know that as little money as you have, you surely have enough to share with her. Your first impulse is to give her some change. There's even a part of you that's ready to reach in your pocket for a little folding money—a one, or even a five. What the heck, make it a grand moment for her. Light her up.*
>
> *Then the thought comes in. What, are you crazy?' We've only got seven dollars to get us through the day! You want to give her five? so you start fumbling around for that one.'*

By the time this inner dialogue has gone on, you've walked past the woman without giving her anything and you missed an opportunity. She gets nothing, and neither do you—you missed the joy of sharing.

To change a core belief, act on your first impulse. You must act quickly, or your intellect will kill the idea before you know it. Remember this, the only difference between you and a bag lady is your thoughts—she has not yet accepted for herself the standard of living that you have today. When you act on your first thought often enough you create a new belief and you learn to trust yourself.

Fear tells us to distrust, love inspires us to give. If you're unsure if you can trust your first thought to be your intuition guiding you, ask yourself if the thought is in alignment with your values. If it is then you can comfortably follow this intuition.

David's Story

When I first heard about acting on your first thought my main concern was how I'd be able to differentiate between intuition and fear. I decided to act on impulses that wouldn't reap any dramatic consequences to begin with.

The following day I was visiting a friend who lived in the Blue Mountains, a two hour journey from my home. My friend had recently moved into a new house, so instead of buying him a house warming present I decided to give him money so he could choose a plant for his garden. While I was waiting at the train station for my friend to pick me up I noticed a nursery next door. I wandered in and was immediately impressed by a beautiful standard rose, my first thought was to buy it for my friend, which I did without hesitation.

My friend was delighted with the gift and when we arrived at his house he showed me the bare spot he'd left in his garden, for the exact rose I'd purchased.

Begin by acting on your first thought on unimportant matters like David did, so that the consequences will not have a dramatic impact on your life. Over time you will learn to differentiate between intuition and fear.

Watch your words

I actively listen to the words people say, these are the clues that tell me what their real beliefs are. One day I noticed how many people, including myself, started their sentences with 'I think'. It's a very common expression. If you are one of many who use this expression stop and think about what you're really saying. Sometimes you might be thinking out loud, but more often than not it's habit, you've become so accustomed to saying it you do so even when it's unnecessary.

Every time you say 'I think', you express a doubt. Just imagine that you say 'I think', or a variation of it such as 'I guess', 'perhaps', 'I'll try', 'possibly' or, 'maybe' hundreds of times a day—what do you think will happen? You'll constantly doubt yourself. Make a conscious effort to eliminate any words that imply doubt from your vocabulary. A lot of the time these words are unnecessary however, if you need to say something in place of 'I'll try' for instance, say 'I'm working on…' instead.

Give thanks in advance

When you reach this step stop saying your statement of truth and give thanks for all that you desire as if you already have them. Giving thanks in advance is one of the most powerful things you can do.

Emily was in a financial predicament and applied to her bank for a loan to help her reorganise her finances however, the bank refused her application. When she contacted me she was very upset. I suggested that she give thanks for the money that she needed without focusing on where the money would come from. At the same time I suggested she apply to a number of other financial institutions for a loan. A week later she emailed me overjoyed at the outcome. Her bank, which had previously refused her a loan, rang and apologised saying they had made a mistake and her loan was approved.

Give thanks before the object of your desire is present in your life, then give thanks after it manifests as well. It's the perfect way to allow no doubt and to break the worry habit at the same time.

A good way to break the worry habit is to give thanks for everything that is good in your life every time you become consciously aware that you are worrying, or thinking negatively. This can include the sun, air, trees, the beauty of nature, your great country. You can give thanks for your home, possessions, friends, intellect, ideas, work and the people that you love, the list is endless, we all have so much to be grateful for.

Decide now not to waste precious time and energy dwelling on something that may never happen.

Allowing no doubt doesn't mean that you'll feel totally confident every minute of the day; it means that you simply don't dwell on the possibility of getting less than what you really want.

Step Nine

Love and respect yourself

The first way we begin to dishonour ourselves is by not telling the truth. The truth about what we feel, what we want, or what we think.

—Iyanla Vanzant

People who don't love and respect themselves often feel powerless. This feeling of inadequacy can manifest as; addictions, money problems, relationship problems, weight issues and even confusion about what you really want.

To go beyond powerlessness to authentic power, you need to understand what loving and respecting yourself really means. Loving yourself doesn't mean simply indulging yourself. Loving and respecting yourself is a life-long process that's not about the achievement of a specific goal, or having nice things—it's about understanding your needs and taking responsibility for fulfilling those needs. It means acknowledging your real feelings and being honest about what you really want and how you really feel.

Know your real needs

It's your responsibility to take whatever steps are necessary to meet your own emotional, physical and spiritual needs. The common emotional needs that we all share are:

We need to love and be loved. For most of us, close personal relationships are our greatest source of happiness, and our greatest source of pain. Choose from your heart by all means but understand that happy, harmonious relationships are not about need fulfillment. Close personal relationships provide you with opportunities, on a daily basis, to choose to be the highest and best of who you are.

Relationships are not about obligations. A relationship that is entered into with the commitment to obtain from the relationship the opportunity to grow, heal every aspect of your life, and demonstrate the highest and best of who you are to each other, is the relationship that will bring you the most happiness.

We need to be honest with ourselves. Iyanla Vanzant author of, *One Day My Soul Just Opened Up*[11] says, 'When you lie to yourself about what you need, you'll eventually lie to others about the same thing. Lying to yourself and others is akin to having a bacterial fungus. It spreads quickly into all areas of your life and pollutes your very being.'

Being honest with yourself about what you want, and how you really feel, is the only way to be free. Instead of being honest we sometimes hide our real desires from ourselves and make excuses, or we blame others. We also hide our pain and sadness behind addictions, feelings of inadequacy and by pretending to be something we're not.

I've seen hundreds, probably thousands, of clients who fill their lives with consolation prizes of possessions and status symbols. You will be able to recognise if you've settled for the consolation prize if you constantly; live beyond your means; live and mix in circles with people who have much more money and freedom than you can afford; have to have a certain standard of living in order to be happy.

I'm not for one moment suggesting that you cannot have friends that are better off than you. The instance I am referring to is when your whole life has been created around living up to an image, usually a false one. This is the easiest thing to deny and justify by saying, 'I just like nice things'.

Answer these questions honestly. Would you:

- move to a different part of town, which means lowering your standard of living for a period of time, say a year or two, if it meant you would be better off financially over the long term?
- be comfortable for others to know your real financial situation?

Do you:

- think you are too good for some menial forms of work, for example; cleaning or street sweeping?
- infer that you are better off than you are?
- feel that you are better than some people?
- feel that you are superior to others?
- feel mad at yourself?
- feel mad at life for giving you such a raw deal?

- blame your husband for not giving you the life you want?
- feel cheated of your rightful heritage?
- feel like a failure when you don't have what you want?
- obsess over what you want until you get it?
- feel tired all the time?

If you answered yes to at least half of these questions you need be aware that your ego is in control, and ego robs you of your power. You can have what you desire in life, but if having your desires means giving up your self-respect you won't be happy even when you get it. Self-respect is feeling good about yourself, and that feeling is not dependent upon the approval of others. When your life is a lie you expend so much energy living up to that lie, that there's not enough energy left over to create the reality you really desire.

One way to change is to ask yourself what's most important to you. If you're willing to break free from the influence of the tribe then you need to be totally honest with yourself and take action to change any limiting beliefs. You don't have to tell everybody your business—you just stop pretending to be something that you're not.

I heard a woman explain one day how she stayed in a physically abusive relationship because she was demonstrating unconditional love. This is a classic case of lying to yourself. By putting up with such behaviour you actually condone and encourage it. Everyone who comes into our lives can be our teacher. If someone teaches us to value ourselves more then they have served their purpose. Forgive them and move on, don't get caught up in their issues.

We need to be valued. It took me many years to realise that being loved did not necessarily mean being valued. When I first became aware that I'd never been valued in my romantic relationships with men, and even with some girlfriends, I thought it was because I'd chosen the wrong people to form relationships with. Later, I came to realise that being valued is about the standards that we set for ourselves. There's a saying I've heard many times, 'We teach people how to treat us'.

Every problem in life is an opportunity and during the time when I was making these discoveries, I was given an opportunity to value myself, and to set a new standard when a client reneged on an agreement to pay me royalties.

The first book that I ghost wrote was for a millionaire businessman. He agreed to pay me a set fee, plus an ongoing royalty payment, based on the number of books sold. The first royalty payment was due six months after the book was released however, when that time came I received nothing. I sent him a friendly reminder which was ignored. I didn't do anything more about it at the time thinking that he was busy and would probably get around to paying me. Six months passed and another payment date came and went with no sign of a cheque. This time I rang him and his accountant. Neither of them returned my calls. So I wrote and faxed, and still my requests were ignored. Under normal circumstance I might have thought that this man didn't sell many books, however I knew he had a reputation for being an outstanding salesman with a multi-million dollar organisation behind him. Even if this was the case he could have returned my calls.

I decided it was a time for me to reassess how I'd been teaching others how to treat me particularly as there had been previous instances when people had taken advantage of me and I hadn't pursued the matter. I chose to take legal action to enforce our contract. While this was not my preferred option, it was an important step that I needed to take in valuing myself at that time.

While all of this was going on I talked about this situation with friends, however it wasn't long before I realised that I was putting myself in the role of the victim, and in making myself right and the other person wrong I wasn't acting like the person that I wanted to be. So I chose to stop talking about this matter and even went so far as to write this man a letter thanking him for all that I had learnt from this experience, and wishing him well.

The matter was eventually settled out of court, and I received a one off payment in lieu of future royalties. However, by this time the amount of money I received was not the issue. I learnt so much about myself through this experience, and I had so many opportunities to change any limiting beliefs.

You can set standards by learning to say no when you don't want to do something. It's not always easy to refuse to do something for someone, particularly when you've spent most of your life pleasing others, but you don't help anyone by doing things you don't want to do and becoming resentful in the process. Unless I am absolutely sure I want to do something I've developed the habit of saying, 'Let me think about it'. This gives me time to decide before making a commitment. However, I will point out that some people use this phrase as a way of avoiding the issue, and it's not a considerate way to act. If you ask for time to think about it always get back to the person with your answer.

The way to change any habit is to begin with small changes, just make sure that as you advance, you step outside your comfort zone. You need to stretch yourself and your belief of what you are capable of doing and having in order live a life you really love. You can do more with your life than you ever dreamed. As you gain confidence in showing people how to treat you in minor matters, you'll find it easier to be honest, and set standards on the really important issues.

At the time of writing this book I'm very overweight. I say 'at this time' because I know it's only a temporary situation, I will be slim again. I've tried to lose weight, I exercise and do so regularly but it's something I haven't mastered yet. There was a time when I didn't want to be in the public eye looking this way because I didn't feel that the way I looked was congruent with what I taught. However, I believe in the principles I'm sharing with you in this book so much that I want to tell the world. So I've chosen to accept this is an opportunity for me to value and accept myself exactly as I am now, and to be independent of what other people may think of me. I am not going to wait until I look perfect to spread this message, because I am good enough now.

Self respect is how you feel about yourself on the inside, not what you have, or how you look on the outside.

We need to love ourselves. Self love is about taking responsibility for filling your own needs, rather than waiting for, or expecting, someone else to do it for you. When you really love yourself you put yourself first. This is not about being selfish—it's the same as putting the oxygen mask on yourself in a plane first, so that you can then help others. You cannot help anyone else until you can look after yourself.

Self love is also about allowing into your life the things that make you happy. I encourage my clients to live the life they really want *now*, to do the things for themselves that they would do when they have everything they want *now*. What still surprises me is how many excuses people make for not making time for themselves. Your life will not suddenly change when you manifest all your desires, you'll still be the same person, so cherish yourself.

We need to accept responsibility for achieving our own goals. Think about this: Respect + Responsibility = Rewards.

When you set standards for how you allow others to treat you, you demonstrate respect for yourself. Add to this responsibility for creating all that you desire and you will know that you can have anything you want. That is what real power is all about.

I have counselled many couples seeking financial advice and in most cases usually one partner carries the burden for the financial management. It's usually this person who makes the appointment to see me, and often they have a hidden agenda—they hope I will encourage their partner to be more responsible, or take a more active role in managing their money. I usually disappoint them because I believe everyone has the right to act in any way they choose; I also know that everyone has to live with the consequences of their choices. The fact is that you can't make anyone act the way that you think they should, no matter how right you may think you are.

We influence others the most by demonstrating our beliefs through our actions. You will get a far more positive response from others, and achieve more by focusing on yourself, who you want to be and how you want to act, rather than wasting energy trying to change another.

One reason we sometimes try to change others is because we mistakenly believe they are holding us back. I have had people say to me, 'You're lucky to be on your own, you don't have a husband who spends all your money (or won't let you do what you want)'. Well, it's not any easier bringing up children on one income and paying for child-care and babysitting every time you want to go out. While I understand that it can be hard to achieve your dreams when one person spends more than their share, or does not support you, no-one is dependant on their partner to survive or to help them achieve their goals. That may sound harsh but until you can accept this you'll limit the opportunities available to you.

You are always responsible for you, and there is always a way to achieve what you want. You don't always need money to achieve your dreams, sometimes there is another way—the most important first step is to believe in yourself, choose who you want to be and what makes you happy, and often the rest just seems to work out. I know that what I'm about to say is contrary to what many financial advisers say however, from my own experience and from observing my clients achieve their goals I've found that money is the least important commodity that you need to achieve your dreams.

When I started my first business, a typing service, I didn't even own a typewriter—I simply told everyone I met that I was running a typing business. When work came along just a couple of days later I borrowed money from a girlfriend to hire a typewriter. In those days I was living on what was officially known as the poverty line so there wasn't a cent left over to promote a business with. However, when I focused on a creating a brochure to promote my services, without getting bogged down in how I could afford it, a man came into my life that provided me with exactly what I wanted.

I was at a party and talking to a man I'd only just met about my small business and I happened to mention that I needed a brochure to advertise my services. Now this man didn't know anything about me or my circumstances and I knew nothing about him. As it turned out he just happened to teach graphic design and printing at TAFE. He suggested, without any prompting on my part, that he have his students design and print a brochure for me as part of their assignment, and he asked me to mail the wording for the brochure to him. True to his word a few weeks later this man dropped off five hundred copies of a top quality brochure, at no charge. This was the only contact I ever had with this man. I don't even remember his name or what he looks like, but I am eternally grateful for his kindness. That brochure brought more clients my way and allowed me to expand my business and improve my standard of living.

We need passion. Passion in this instance is not about romance—it's about doing something that you love. Doing work that's your passion is a great way to live, but if that's not possible at this time, then add something into your life that you're passionate about; it could be a hobby, sport, or volunteer work. Passion is what makes you feel glad to be alive for no particular reason at all.

We need time to connect with our spirit. Too much busyness, and always 'doing' takes you away from inner peace. It's easy to forget that life is not just about the achievement of goals, getting through the day, looking after a family, or doing your job. By taking time out to connect with your spirit you remember what's really important to you, and you experience peace. Life is merely a process of remembering, over and over again.

We need balance. You cannot expect one area of your life to fulfil all of your needs. For instance, when you first fall in love everything seems wonderful, but this time doesn't last forever—when the honeymoon period ends it doesn't mean that you are any less in love.

Some people, after being in a relationship for awhile feel discontented and often they wonder what's gone wrong with the relationship—when all that feeling of discontent means, is that it's time to create balance in another area of your life.

John Gray, author of How To Get What You Want And Want What You Have[12], refers to our emotional needs as love tanks, in this book John says:

> *When a tank is filling up, we experience an increase in positive feeling. At those filling-up times, we may think it is our partners who make us happy, but it is actually the joy of connecting with our inner selves that makes us happy. Yet our partners' love and support allows us to get back to ourselves.*
>
> *When someone sees or treats us with love, we are then better able to connect to who we are. The different kinds*

of love help us to connect with different facets of who we are.

When a love tank is completely full, the symptom is not continuous fulfillment. Instead, it is often boredom or restlessness and then dissatisfaction. Although we may think we are dissatisfied with our partners, we are actually feeling the collective emptiness of other tanks...

When couples were not getting along, I would first recommend doing something to fill up their other love tanks.

This principle not only applies to relationships it can apply to all areas of our lives. Sometimes we put too much of ourselves into our work, or our children. So, remember that when you feel dissatisfied it may mean that it's time to create more balance. It may be all you need to re-establish your equilibrium.

Filling your own needs is not something that you do once, it's something that needs to be done on a regular basis.

We need to trust. Fulfilling your own needs is about trusting yourself and your ability to fill those needs. You need to be able to trust yourself, before you can trust someone else, or even trust God. The following are some thoughts on trust.

Trust is patient. When you know you can have everything you desire and it's just a matter of time before it manifests, you know that you can wait for those things that may be out of your reach right now.

Trust is knowing that you are always good enough. No matter what others may say or imply, you know that you deserve to have your heart's desires.

Trust is knowing that you are okay just the way you are. You don't have to look a certain way, or live a certain way in order to be acceptable, or prove anything.

Trust is refusing to allow others to abuse you. You know that you'll always love yourself, therefore you can set standards and act in a way that states clearly that you won't accept abuse in any form.

Trust is making time for the things that you enjoy regularly. When you know there will always be enough for you and you don't have to work all the time, or be perfect, then you can treat yourself as lovingly as you would your soul mate.

Trust is acting even when you feel doubtful. Trust is just like a muscle, you develop it by trusting.

Trust is also the foundation of all good relationships. You need to learn to trust yourself first, before you can expect it from others. As you learn to love, respect and trust yourself you will automatically attract to you people who are trustworthy.

Change what you can and accept what you can't

Throughout this book I have advocated change as a way to create a life you love; it's not my intention to suggest that you are not okay exactly as you are. You don't have to be perfect to have what you want. It's more important to accept yourself as you are, and that means flaws and all. Sometimes we have issues that take longer than we prefer to master and that's okay. It is better to love and accept yourself exactly as you are right now than to place conditions on self love.

Step Ten

You can have everything you want when you don't need it

No-one ever finds life worth living he has to make it worth living

—Unknown

The hardest thing for most of us to do is to let go—yet it's this very action that will draw all that you desire into your life. It's not uncommon when you really, really, want something to think about it all the time, until the thought of it consumes your waking hours. You may talk about it to others, plan for it, and live for the day when your dream becomes a reality, but often these actions can sabotage your efforts.

When you want something too much, when your happiness depends upon the achievement of goals, then fear and doubt have a fertile breeding ground. Before long fear-filled thoughts of worry and doubt can enter your consciousness, and soon after your focus shifts from what you want, to worrying about whether or when, you will obtain it—or worse still, to trying to make it happen.

Marie's story

After the birth of my son I took on a part-time position as a telemarketer. Each week I was expected to achieve a certain number of appointments and most weeks I was able to do so. After reading Financially Free I set a goal to increase the number of appointments I made so that I would make more money. The first week I achieved this goal easily. However, by the second week of focusing on the goal, I didn't make any appointments whatsoever.

I was confused as to what I was doing wrong. When I was talking to potential clients I felt as if they were about to make an appointment, that they wanted to say yes, and yet they didn't.

When Anne explained that I was trying too hard and focusing on myself, rather than on helping the other person, it clicked. So, I changed my approach. I made a conscious choice at the beginning of each day as to how many appointments I'd like to make. For the rest of the day I didn't give that goal another thought. I focused on helping others and having fun.

With this approach I broke all of my own records. However, little did I know at the time that this problem would lead me to my passion. I did the very first Ten Step course that Anne ran and loved it. Months later Anne rang and told me she was teaching others to be life coaches and suggested that I would be suitable. I knew instantly it was what I wanted to do.

I love life coaching and now I conduct courses myself and I have built a successful practice. In building up this business I've continually needed to remind myself to let go. Whenever I get too intense and try to make things happen the phone stops ringing. I've discovered that the more I relax and let it happen, at the same time having a very clear intention of what I want and taking the appropriate action to let people know I'm in business, my business grows.

You really can have everything that you want when you focus on making others happy.

You know that when the seeds are in the ground in your garden you can't see them, that doesn't mean they aren't growing. When seedlings appear you can see them although they are still tiny and vulnerable, and not yet like the flowers they will become once in full bloom. If you gave up your life to stand guard and watch these seedlings grow you would miss a good deal of life and its pleasures. Yet this is precisely what you do when you obsess over what you want by thinking about it all the time and trying to work out ways to achieve your goals—you miss out on enjoying everyday life.

Your thoughts and words are like food and water you give your plants. Feed your dreams regularly with thoughts, words and actions that support that dream—then get on with your life. You won't achieve your dreams any faster by obsessing.

Obsession is akin to pulling out the seedlings everyday to see if the roots are growing. If you continued to do this all of your plants would eventually die.

There are some people who think and act positively, but still struggle to achieve their goals. I believe that it's because they haven't really detached from the outcome.

When you think about what you want all of the time, your focus is on *getting*. When you support your goals with positive thoughts and actions and then focus on *giving* as Marie did, you will achieve your goals easily and effortlessly.

Be the person you want to be now

When I was developing and working with these Ten Steps my life improved dramatically. However, it wasn't until I made a major decision that I was finally free. I decided that I wasn't going to wait another day to be the person that I wanted to be, or *do* the things that I wanted to do for myself and for others. Like a lot of people there were things that I wanted to do *one day*, and these were things that I had put off doing until I had more money and time—in other words until I achieved my personal goals.

Commitment versus ego

Think about what commitment means for you, and ask yourself if you are really committed to your dream, or is your ego holding you back?

I have seen many people over the years that I know could have succeeded easily, if they'd only been able to put their egos aside. When you dictate how you will achieve your goals, or limit what you will do to achieve them, your choices are usually governed by your ego.

Another client believed that she was totally committed to developing and building her business as she'd spent money on credit that she didn't yet have, or had little possibility of raising. I must admit there have been times in the past when I've done the same until I realised this behaviour was actually taking me away from what I really wanted.

When you stop and think about the consequences of such an action it often means that if your idea doesn't work, then you expect someone else to take responsibility for you and pick up the tab. Or, more likely you've never thought about the consequences. This behaviour is not to be confused with allowing no doubt, which means allowing no doubt in a responsible way. We always need to be prepared to accept the consequences of our actions. This behaviour is a prime example of how we try to make things happen, and it's usually an act of desperation, not commitment.

When you try to make things happen, you act out of fear.

How committed are you? If it was necessary would you:

- clean houses?
- be a labourer?
- sweep streets?
- stay in a job you hate?
- take any job?
- get up an hour earlier?
- study?

- do what you love for nothing, while working at another job?

If you answered 'yes' to most of the above, you're committed. That commitment will help you achieve your goals. If you answered 'no' to most of them you need to reassess if the needs of your ego are more important than achieving your goal, and usually that's because you are still bonded to the tribe.

One person experiencing financial difficulties might say they would do anything to avoid losing their home, while another wouldn't even talk about it, they would just go out and obtain any type of work to ensure it didn't happen. There's a big difference between talking and doing. When you won't even contemplate an alternative way of achieving your dream, you know that your ego is running your life.

When your ego controls your choices and actions, you *need* to achieve your goals. When you have a dream, and you're prepared to do whatever is necessary to achieve it, but at the same time you also know that you could live quite happily without it—you will manifest that dream.

Choose what you want then ensure that your daily habits support those choices, then get on with life. This stage of getting on with it with faith is an important one because *what you desire you attract, what you need you repel.*

The question to ask yourself is; how would you live if you knew it was just a matter of time before you had everything that you wanted? Think about what you would do for others, and for the world. Everyone can transform their life through simple, everyday acts of kindness.

Spreading the kindness message

The Kindness Movement was launched in America, the objective being to promote kindness. Anne Herbert, a journalist, coined the phrase, 'Random kindness and senseless acts of beauty' in 1982, you may have seen it on a car bumper sticker. Since that time the Kindness Movement has taken off and now a Kindness week, or day, is held in many countries around the world.

In Australia Brian Willis set up the Australian Kindness Movement, this organisation is non-religious, non-political and is staffed by volunteers. They promote kindness three hundred and sixty five days a year.

Brian first became interested in kindness when a friend gave him the book, *More Random Acts of Kindness* and this acted as a catalyst for Brian to do something more. Brian says, 'I used to read about doing something worthy and I would think, ah yes, but they had contacts, or money, or a university education, and any number of reasons to justify to myself why I couldn't have done something like that. Yet when we really believe in something, we seem to have a corner on the miracle market. It saddens me that many people believe they are powerless'.

If you have not yet tried practising random acts of kindness, you may wish to try one of the following:

- Mow the grass strip in front of your neighbour's house
- Feed an unknown person's expired parking meter
- Donate blood
- Praise a fellow worker

- Slip a few dollars, discreetly, into the pocket of a needy person
- Drop coins in an area where children play
- Write to a company if an employee has been helpful
- Buy a fellow worker a cup of coffee
- Put your shopping trolley back where it belongs
- Send cash anonymously in the mail to someone for no reason at all
- Allow someone into your traffic lane
- Allow someone to have your parking spot
- Tell someone just how great you think they are
- Send someone a letter telling them what an impact they've had on your life
- Let someone in ahead of you at the supermarket check-out
- Pick up someone else's garbage
- Pay for an extra movie ticket and ask the ticket seller to give it to someone in the queue anonymously
- Buy a friend, family member or fellow worker flowers for no reason at all
- Offer to help someone with their job
- Help someone else to get a promotion
- Tell your boss about someone else's good performance
- Don't complain—encourage change that benefits everyone

- Say thank you often
- Smile a lot

I can guarantee you the feeling of wellbeing that you'll receive from performing simple acts of generosity towards another, can change your life. I urge you to try it.

Love the life you live

It's time now to stop dreaming and to start living a life that you love. If you have a dream you have it for a reason and you have the power within you to create it. The process of creating a life you love is simple, but it's not always easy. It takes practise to change the habits of a lifetime, to stop yourself from reacting in the same old way, and to master new habits that support your choices.

The Ten Steps aren't something that you practise just once, they are a lifetime commitment. However, the more you live them, the easier they become and the day will come when practising them is so natural you won't even have to think about it. If at any time you feel stuck, or confused, I suggest that you go back over these steps because I know that if you work with them they can transform your life.

It's you and no-one else who decides what your life will be. Letting go doesn't mean giving up your dream, although it may mean that you let go of how and when you will achieve it.

My wish for you is that you create love, success, joy and happiness beyond your wildest dreams.

Postscript

I spent the first fifty years of my life looking for love and success outside myself. I once believed that if the right man loved me, if I a made a large amount of money, or if I achieved public recognition that I would be successful and therefore happy—I achieved some of those goals but they didn't make me happy.

On my fiftieth birthday I decided to spend the rest of my life living in service to others. In giving to others I found myself, and my reason for being. I discovered that I already had everything I needed and that happiness comes from within, not from other people or material possessions.

Living the Ten Steps in this book, and focusing on serving others had a profound impact on my life. I no longer have the void within me that I once sought to fill.

I love the life I live and in the process of creating it I also gained inner peace, which is far more satisfying than the achievement of material goals.

I urge you to consider living your life in service to others *now*.

What you do for your self, you do for another.
What you do for another, you do for your self.
Conversations with God—Neale Donald Walsch

Anne Hartley

Bibliography

All of the books referred to in this section are highly recommended.

1. Caroline Myss, *Anatomy of the Spirit*, Bantam Books, New York, 1996.
2. Betty Shine, *Mind Waves*, Bantam Books, London, 1993.
3. Louise Samways, *Your MindBody Energy*, Viking O'Neill, Melbourne, 1992.
4. Paul Ka'ikena Pearsall, Linda G.S. Russek, Gary E.R. Schwartz, *The Heart's Code*, Broadway Books, 1998.
5. Caroline Myss, *Why People Don't Heal And How They Can*, Three Rivers Press, New York, 1997.
6. Colin C. Tipping, *Radical Forgiveness*, Gateway, Dublin, 2000.
7. Wayne Dyer, *Dyer Down Under* (cassette program), Nacson Promotions, Sydney, 1998.
8. Wayne Dyer, *Meditations for Manifesting*, Hay House, USA, 1995.
9. Wayne Dyer, *Manifest Your Destiny*, Harper Collins, Sydney, 1997.
10. Neale Donald Walsch, *Conversations with God*, Hodder Stoughton, Sydney, 1995.
11. Iyanla Vanzant, *One Day My Soul Just Opened Up*, Fireside, New York, 1998.
12. John Gray, *How to Get What You Want and Want What You Have*, MacMillan, Sydney, 1999.

Index

About Anne Hartley and Hart Life Coaching

Anne Hartley is the founder of Hart Life Coaching (a division of Hart Publishing Pty Ltd). The purpose of this business is to empower individuals so that they can create a life they really love.

We believe that when we work together for the greater good of all, we achieve more and more people benefit. To this end we train individuals to be life coaches, who in turn can use our material and resources with their individual clients. We are not a franchise organisation and we do not take a percentage of our graduates income. Coaches trained by us conduct their own businesses.

Our core training program, The Ten Steps, was created by Anne Hartley. Anne, who is best known for her work with money issues, at one time owned a women's investment advisory business. During this time she developed a course known as *Financially Free,* which focused on changing attitudes to money as well as habits. This later developed into the best-selling book *Financially Free.*

Anne has spent more than thirty years studying, researching and applying self-development principles to her own life, then sharing them with clients and book readers. As a single parent, seeking to create a better life, she started four small businesses (sometimes without any start up capital), and sold all of them at a profit.

During the early nineties Anne found that while she'd achieved many of her personal goals, they did not make her happy. She spent the next few years searching for a way to create a life that she loved. This search resulted in The Ten

Step program. Anne began sharing these steps with her personal clients and this led to the development of Hart Life Coaching, the training organisation.

If you are looking for a life coach

Anne coaches a limited number of clients either on a casual or regular basis. She can be contacted on the number listed below.

The life coaches listed in the following pages are all accredited by Hart Life Coaching and are trained to work with the Ten Step program. Other accredited life coaches can be found on our web page www.hartlifecoaching.com.au , or you can contact our office.

If you are interested in becoming a life coach

All of our training programs are conducted over the phone in groups using teleconferencing facilities, or individually. Individual training can be done face-to-face, by phone, or by correspondence. This means that distance is no object. Our intention is to have many like-minded coaches assisting individuals throughout the world to create a life they really love.

For more information about our life coach training program, please visit our website www.hartlifecoaching.com.au, or you can contact our office.

Hart Life Coaching
PO Box 769 Mona Vale 2103
Australia Telephone: (0061) 2 9940 1575
Fax: (0061) 2 9940 2091
Email: hart@hartlifecoaching.com.au

Resources

We have a number of products that can assist you to create a life you love.

The Psychology of Money

Anne Hartley

Discover the secrets of successful people. This book is full of inspirational stories about real people who have achieved their dreams.

$19.95 including GST

Love The Life You Live Workbook

This comprehensive workbook includes notes and exercises on the Ten Steps, that you can use to help you create a life you love.

$25.00 including GST

Love The Life You Live cassette program

Reading a book is part of the process, to make it a part of your daily life you need to hear it over and over again. This cassette program, recorded by Anne Hartley, will help you establish new habits so that you too can create a life you love. $19.95 including GST

A revised version of Anne Hartley's best-selling book Financially Free will be available in 2001.

All of the abovementioned products are available from:

Hart Publishing Pty Ltd (ABN 52 002 391 086)
PO Box 769 Mona Vale 2103 Australia
Telephone: (0061) 2 9940 1575
Fax: (0061) 2 9940 2091
Email: hart@hartlifecoaching.com.au

Contact List

We highly recommend Craig Townsend's *Mind Mastery, 12 Minute Daily Relaxation*. This is available from our accredited life coaches, or you can contact:

It's Mind Over Matter
P O Box 106 Belrose West NSW 2085
Telephone: 02 9453 9444
Facsimile: 02 9453 9475
Email: mindmastery@hotmail.com

Support the Australian Kindness Movement by joining for just $20 per year. You can contact them on:

The Australian Kindness Movement can be contacted at:
P O Box 271
Milsons Point NSW 2061
Telephone: 02 9437 5300
Facsimile: 02 9436 1327
Email: kindness@ozemail.com.au
www.kindness.com.au

Hart Publishing Order Form

Please send me the items indicated below. I have enclosed a cheque/money order/bank draft for overseas, made payable to Hart Publishing for $A__________(please include $A2 for postage and packing within Australia or $A5 for international orders) or I have provided my credit card details below.

____copies of The Psychology of Money *by Anne Hartley*	$19.95 inc. GST
____copies of Love The Life You Live Workbook	$25.00 inc. GST
____copies of Love The Life You Live Cassette Program	$19.95 inc. GST

All prices are in Australian Dollars.

Name ____
(PLEASE PRINT CLEARLY)

Address ____

State ____________ Postcode ____________

Home Ph ____________ Wk Ph ____________

E-mail ____________ Fax ____________

Please charge $A__________to my ☐Bankcard ☐Visa ☐Mastercard ☐Amex

Card Number ____________ Expiry Date ____ / ____

Name on Card ____

Signature ____

For overseas orders please add $A5 extra for postage.

Hart Publishing Pty Ltd (ABN 52 002 391 086)

PO Box 769

Mona Vale 2103

Australia

Telephone: (0061) 2 9940 1575

Fax: (0061) 2 9940 2091

Email: hart@hartlifecoaching.com.au

If you would like to go on our mailing list for information about future inspirational products please write or email us.

About David

David is a motivational speaker spreading his message of HOPE. His presentations cover personal empowerment; outstanding customer service and sales. David's mottos is, "Always have hope but forget 'hopefully'. When you allow doubt it never happens'.

David began his career as an actor after being given a scholarship to study at The Ensemble Theatre in Sydney. He later gravitated to the business world and found his niche as manager of the 'Don Burrows Supper Club' before moving on to become a corporate trainer. For many years David travelled the country presenting successful seminars on Excellence in Customer Service, and Sales Techniques.

Ill health finally forced David to give up his training role and the following few years were focused on creating health and conquering the AIDS virus. When David was told by his specialist that he was immune to nearly all drugs available, and that there was only one last drug available to him, he made a commitment to allow no doubt that he would be completely healed.

Just two months later David's doctor said the words that he had waited sixteen years to hear, that the AIDS virus was no longer detectable in his body.

David can be contacted through the office of Hart Publishing Pty Ltd. Telephone: 02 9940 1575, email: hart@hartlifecoaching.com.au